The Robert Pace Keyboard Approach

Book 1
Revised

Music for Piano

Robert Pace

Music for Piano Book 1 Revised

Lee Roberts Music Publications, Inc.
East Greenbush, NY

Distributed By
HAL•LEONARD CORPORATION
7777 W. Bluemound Rd. P.O. Box 13819 Milwaukee, WI 53212

UP AND DOWN

1. Sing the finger numbers for either hand as you "shape" the melody pattern in the air.

MELODY PATTERN
Left Hand

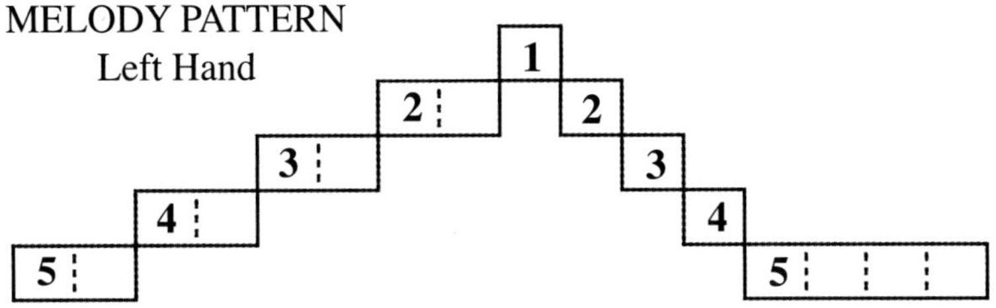

MELODY PATTERN
Right Hand

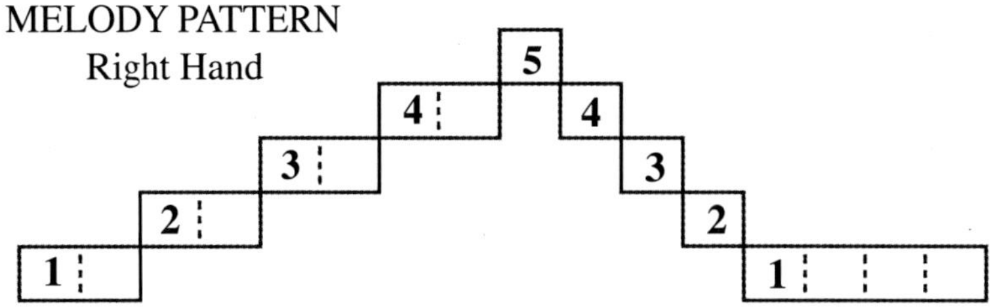

2. Next, clap the rhythm as you sing the finger number.
3. Again, sing each number as you play this on your arm.
4. Finally, play it on the piano keyboard, as you sing the finger number.

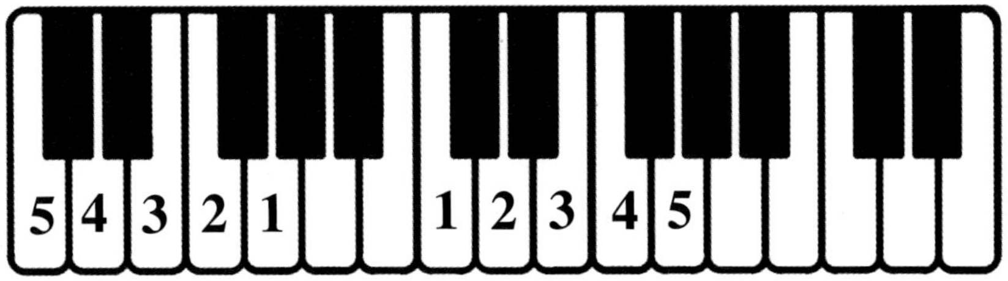

5. Here is another place on the white keys to play "Up and Down."

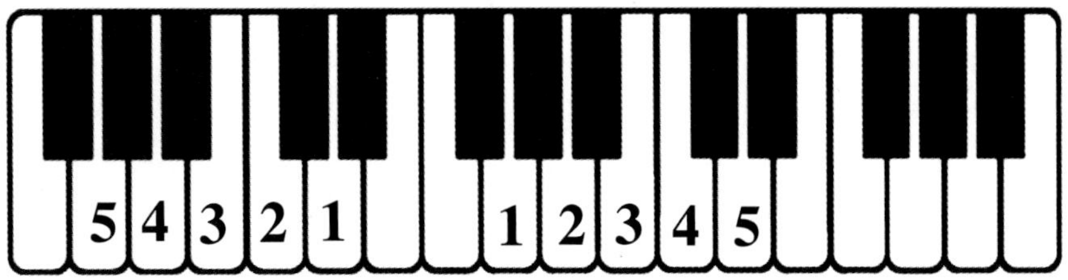

Left Hand

Teacher's Music

Right Hand

SKIPS

This melody pattern "skips" up then down, since it uses only every other tone.
Again:

1. Sing the finger numbers for either hand as you "shape" the melody pattern in the air.
2. Next clap the rhythm as you sing the finger number.
3. Sing each number as you play this on your arm.
4. Finally, play it on the piano keyboard, as you sing the finger number.

MELODY PATTERN
Left Hand

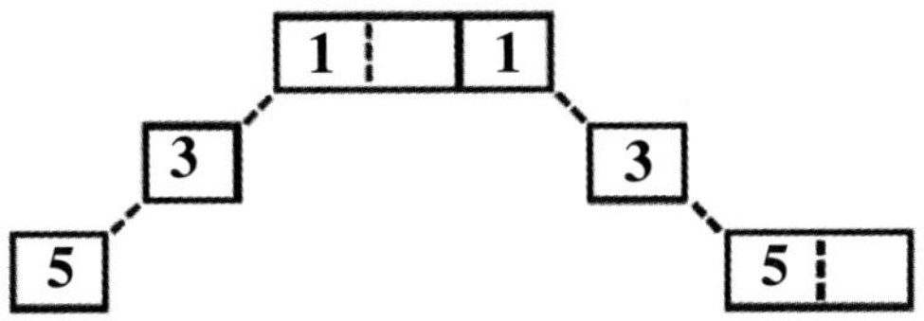

MELODY PATTERN
Right Hand

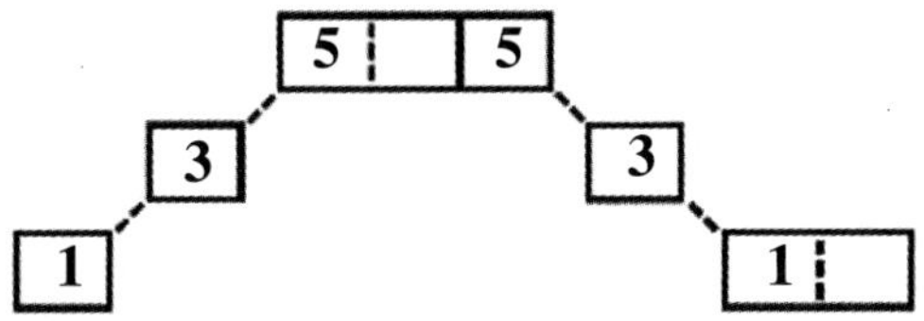

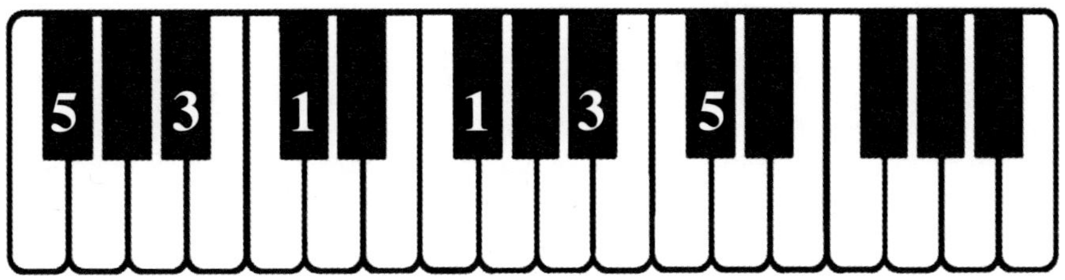

5. Using only the white keys shown here, play "Skips" again

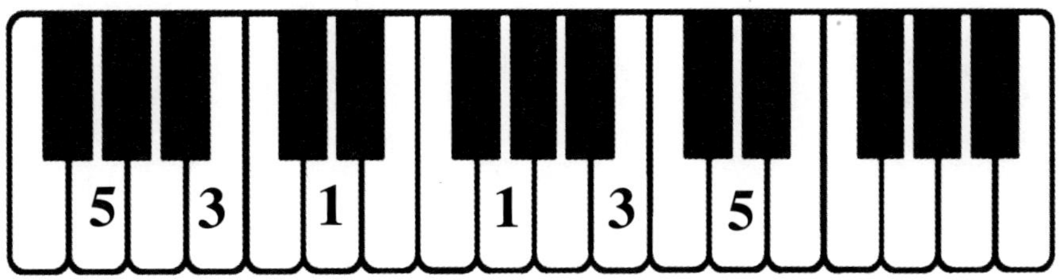

Left Hand

Teacher's Music

Right Hand

SKIPS AND STEPS

1. Each day "shape" the melody pattern in the air as you sing the finger numbers. Also, notice the skips, the repeated pattern and the steps.
2. Find your place on the keyboard, then sing and play the finger numbers.

MELODY PATTERN
Left Hand

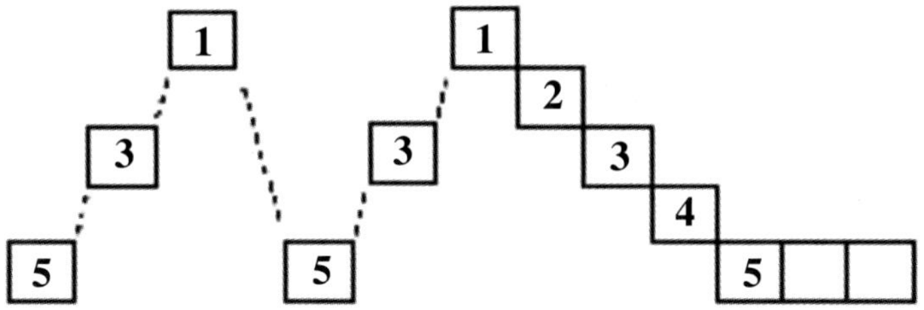

MELODY PATTERN
Right Hand

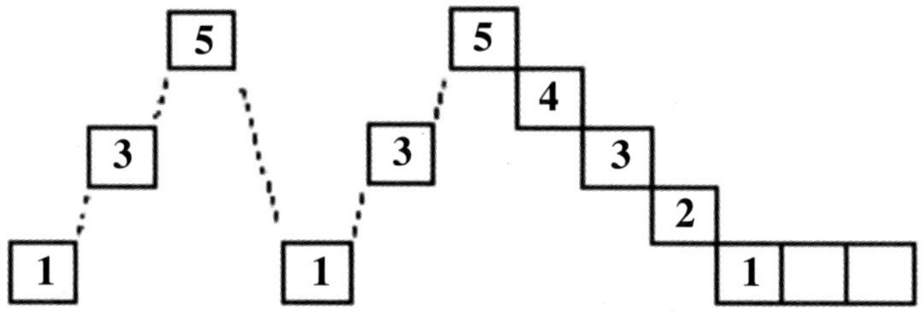

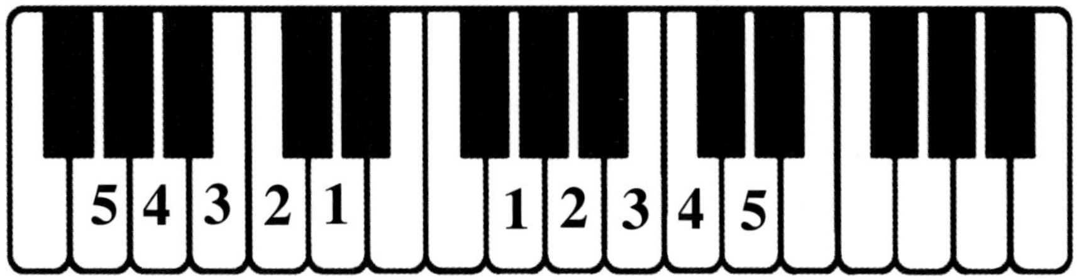

3. Play "Skips and Steps" again on these keys.

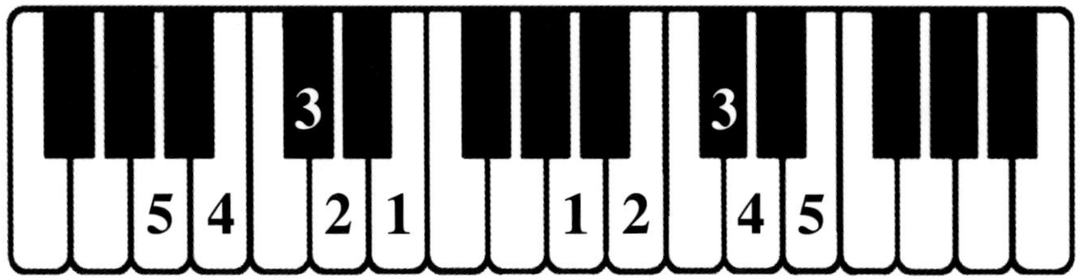

Left Hand

Teacher's Music

Right Hand

SWINGING

Do this each day:

1. Sing the finger numbers as you "shape" the melody pattern in the air. Notice the steps and one repeated tone.
2. Feel the "swing" of the melody as you sing the numbers and play it on the piano keyboard.

MELODY PATTERN
Left Hand

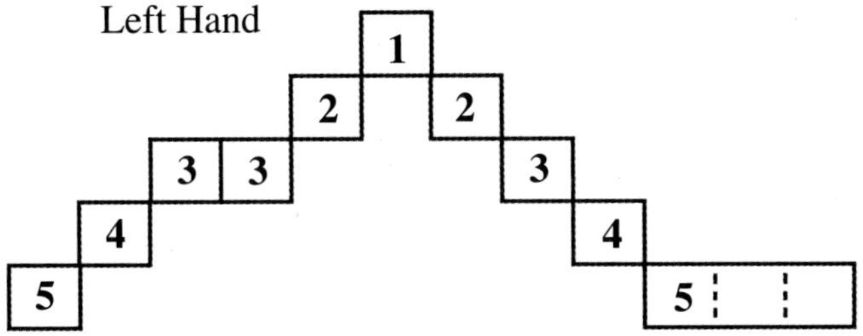

MELODY PATTERN
Right Hand

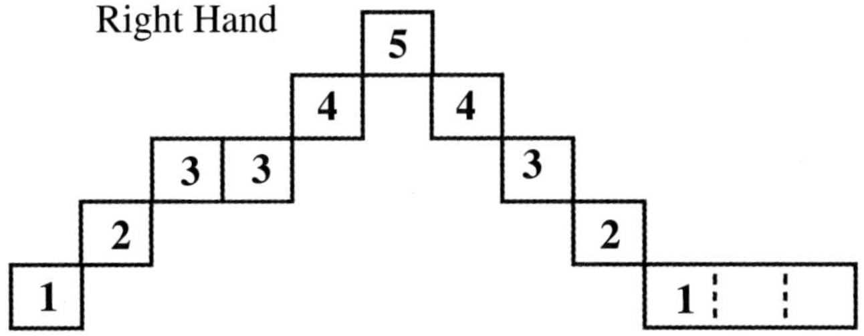

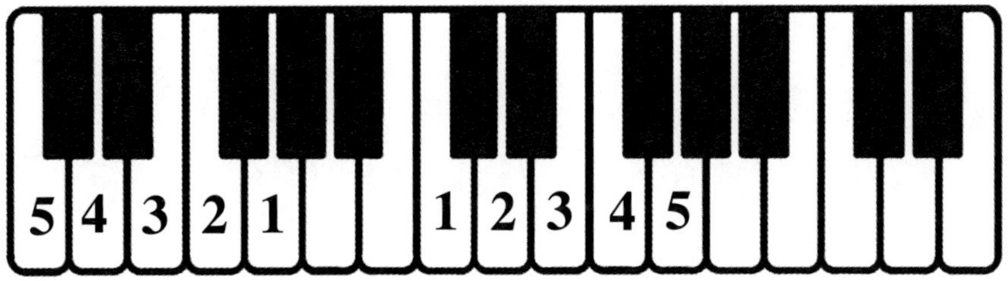

3. To play "swinging" in another place, move each finger to the right and put your 3rd finger on a black key.

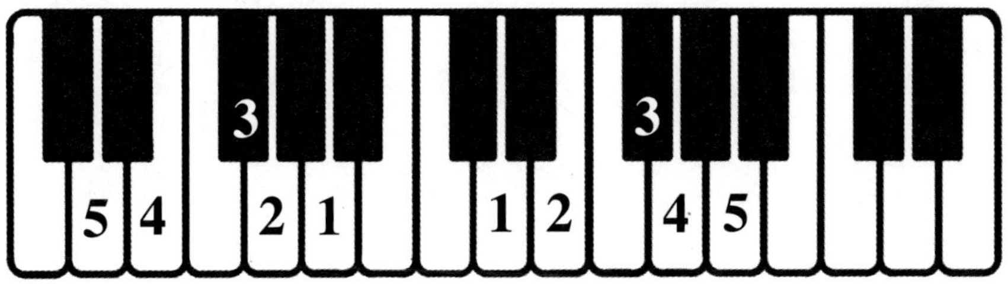

Left Hand

Teacher's Music

Right Hand

OLD WOMAN

1. Notice the skips, repeated pattern, repeated notes, and steps as you sing the finger numbers and shape the melody pattern in the air.
2. Play this on your piano keyboard as you sing the finger numbers.

MELODY PATTERN
Left Hand

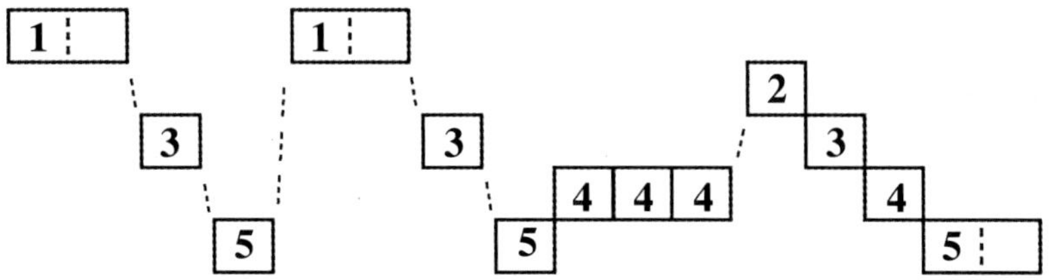

MELODY PATTERN
Right Hand

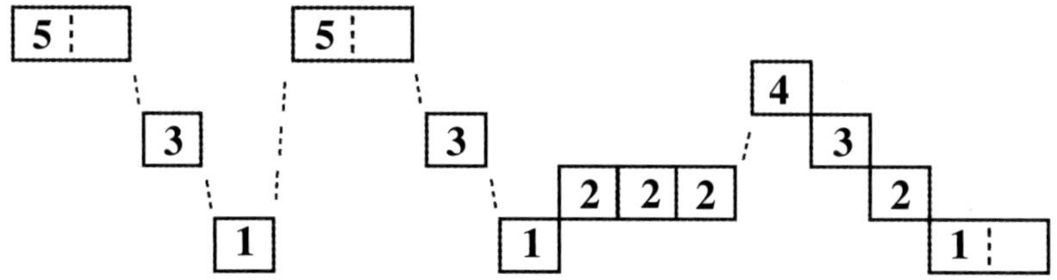

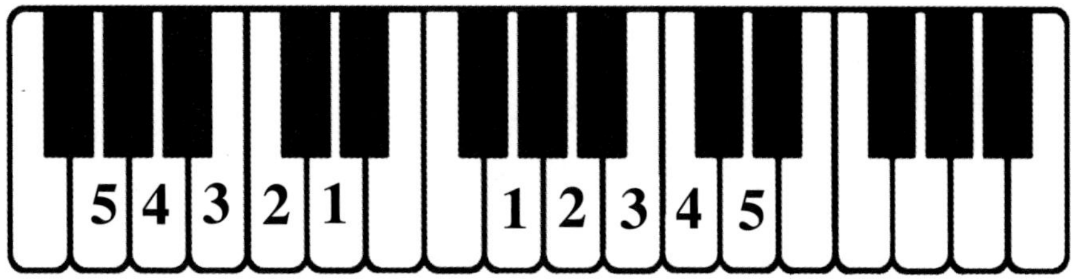

3. Move your fingers to the left to play "Old Woman" again.

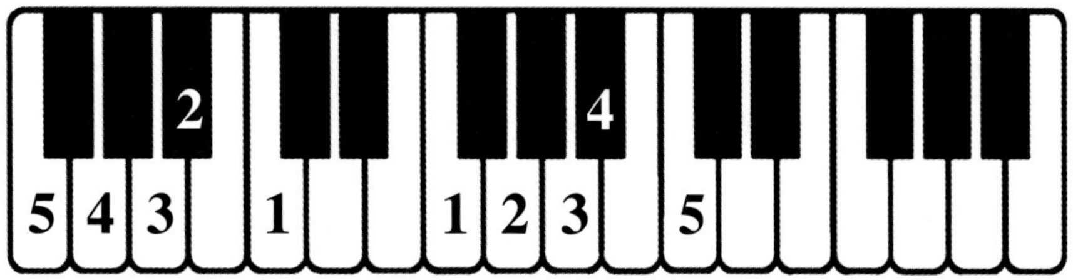

Left Hand

Teacher's Music

Right Hand

OLD MAN

1. Sing the finger numbers and "shape" the melody pattern in the air.
2. Next clap the rhythm as you sing the finger number.
3. Again, sing each number as you play this on your arm.
4. Finally, play it on the piano keyboard, as you sing the finger number.

MELODY PATTERN
Left Hand

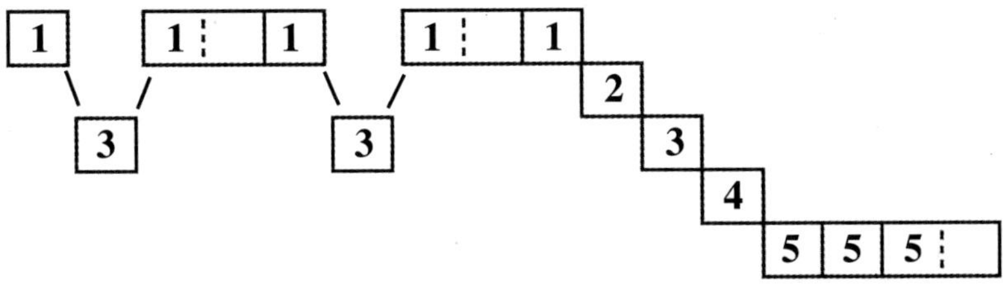

MELODY PATTERN
Right Hand

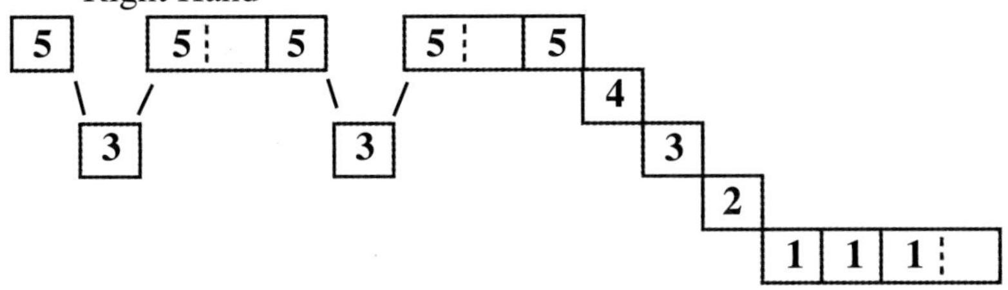

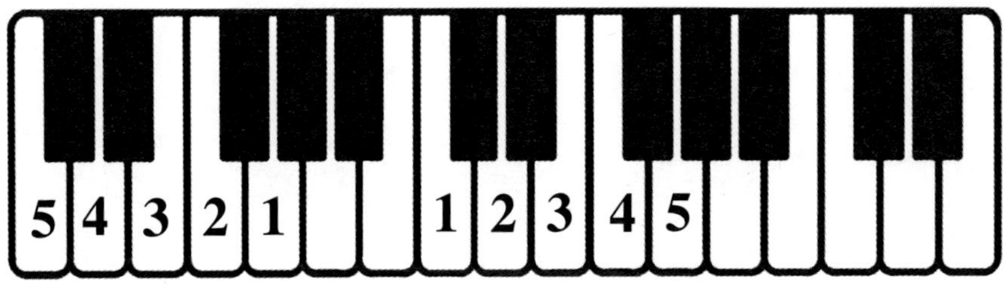

5. Now slide each finger up to the black key just above your 3rd finger on a white key.

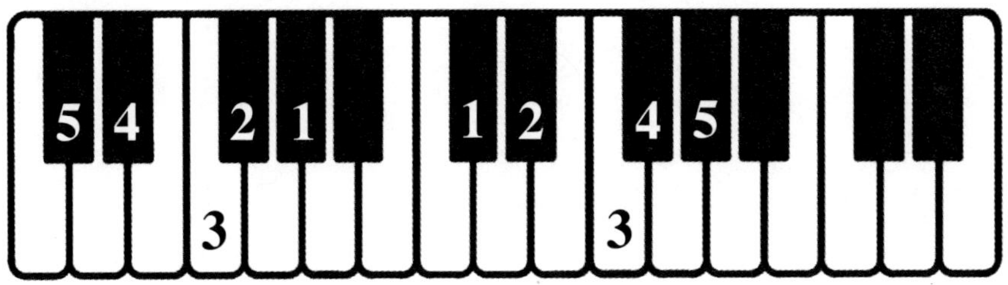

6. See how many different places you can play the songs you have learned so far. You can play "Up and Down" first to help you find the right tones to use.

Left Hand

Teacher's Music

Right Hand

THE GRAND STAFF

The letter names of the piano keyboard go from A to G. Play all of the A's, B's, C's, etc.

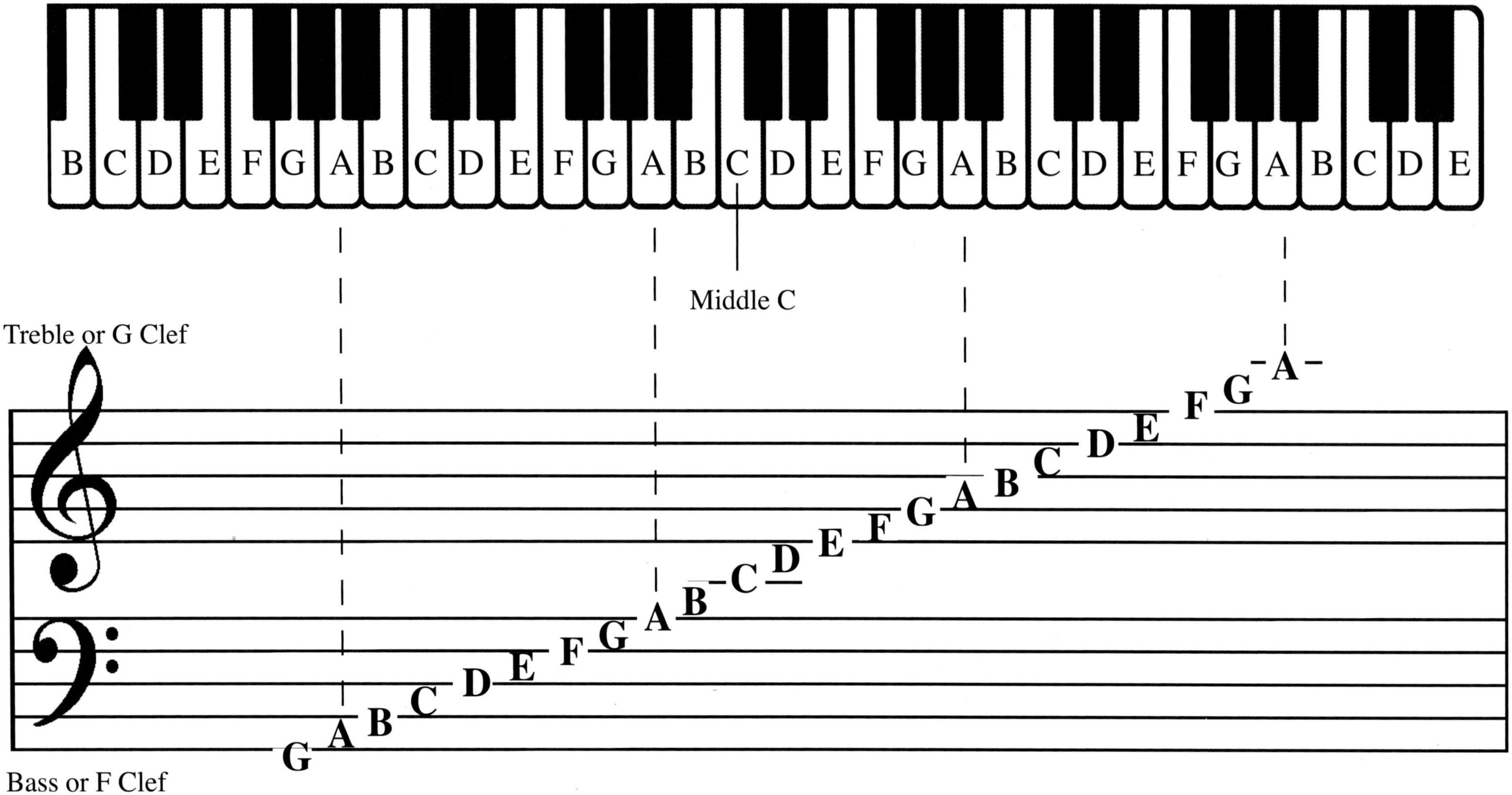

This is the *grand staff*. Learn the letter name of each line and space. Find each on your piano.

MUSICAL NOTATION

Now you are ready to *read* music. Learn to recognize notes and remember how many counts each one gets.

A Quarter Note
gets one count

A Half Note
gets two counts

TIME SIGNATURES

You have already played "Skips" on page 3, so now look at the notation and time signature. Keep your eyes on the notes and sing, *quar-ter, quar-ter, half note* as you play.

SKIPS

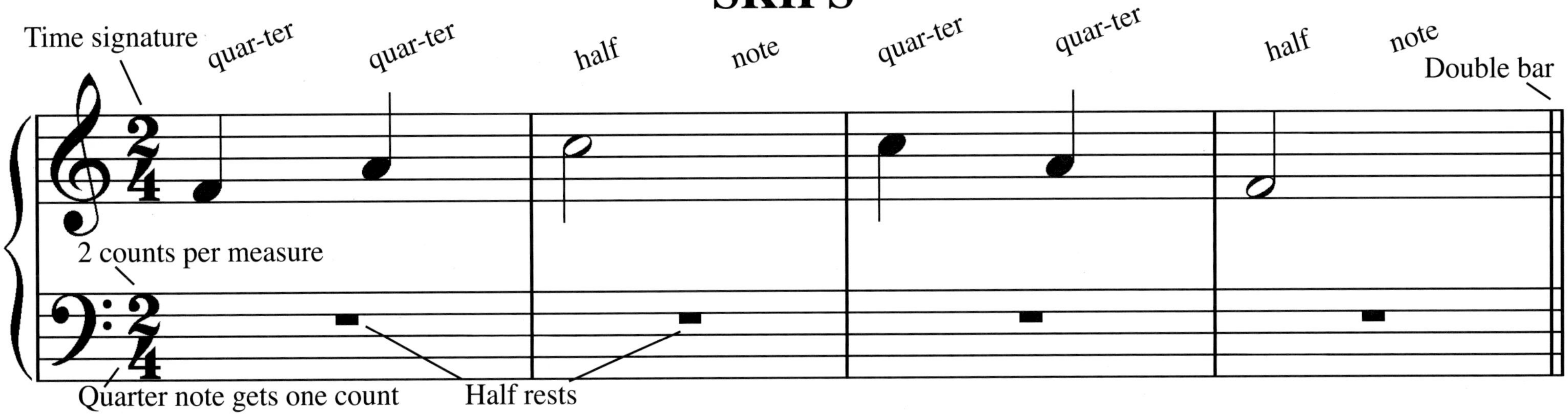

TIME SIGNATURES

We also use the dotted half note (𝅗𝅥.) and the whole note (𝅝) in music. Play “Swinging” with the left hand and chant the note names (quar-ter, etc.). Then do the same as you play “up and down.”

A Dotted Half Note gets three counts

A Whole Note gets four counts

SWINGING

UP AND DOWN

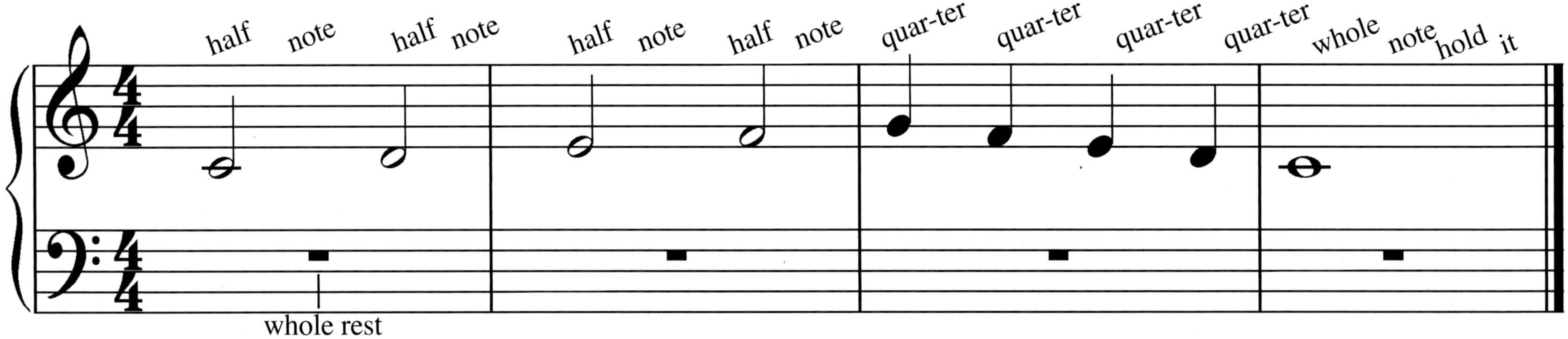

SHARPS

1. SHARPS are made by moving up to the very next key. All sharps are black keys except B# and E#.

FLATS

FLATS are made by moving down to the very next key. All flats are black keys except Cb and Fb.

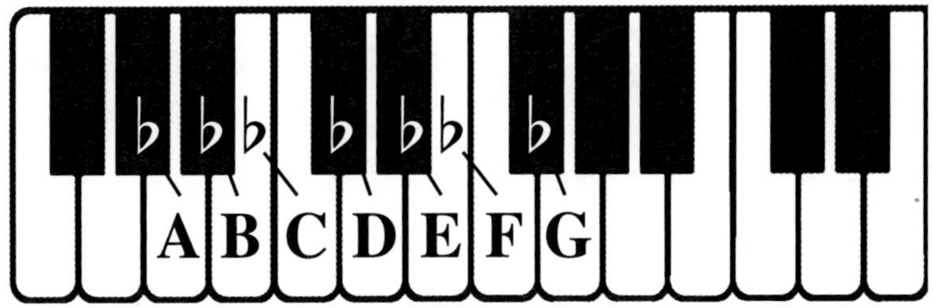

KEY SIGNATURES

2. Place your right thumb on F#, the key-note and play "Up and Down" in the key of F# Major.

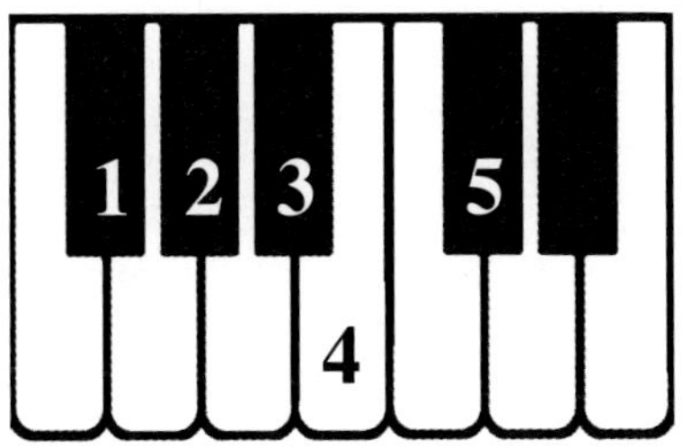

Place your right thumb on Gb, the key-note, and play "Up and Down"in the key of Gb Major.

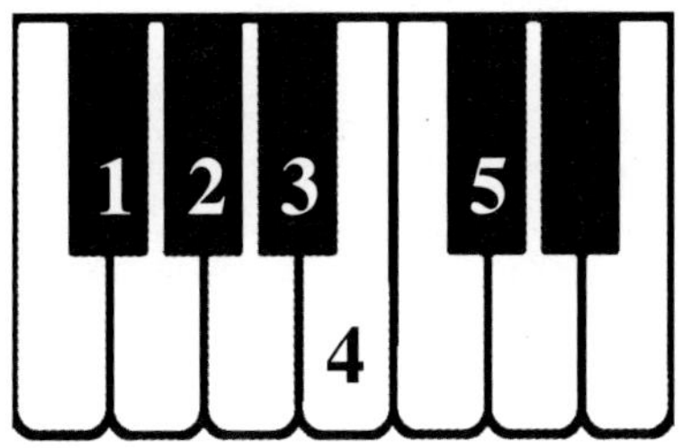

3. To name sharp key signatures: look at the **last sharp** and count up one letter. This is the **key-note**. The key of C Major has no sharps or flats.

To name flat key signatures: find the **next to the last flat**. This is the **key-note**. The key of F Major has one flat.

SKIPS AND STEPS

Each day as you practice "Skips and Steps," ask yourself:
1. Which measures are repeated?
2. Where does the melody skip?
3. Where does it move by steps?

Key of D Major

SKIPS AND STEPS

(Variation)

4. This variation is slightly different. Circle the changes, then each day as you play, change a note or two in one measure to make up a new tune.

AMERICAN FOLK SONG

5. Move your fingers to the right to play this in the key of Eb Major then move them again and play it in E Major.

OLD WOMAN

1. Where does the melody skip?
2. Which measures have repeated tones?
3. Where does the melody move by steps?

FOLK SONG

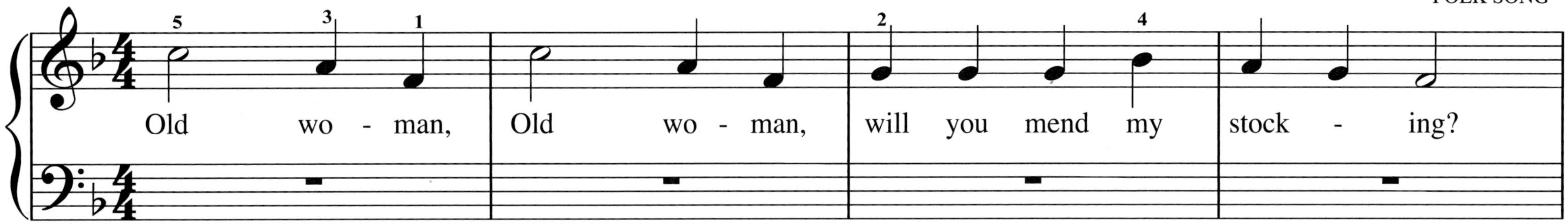

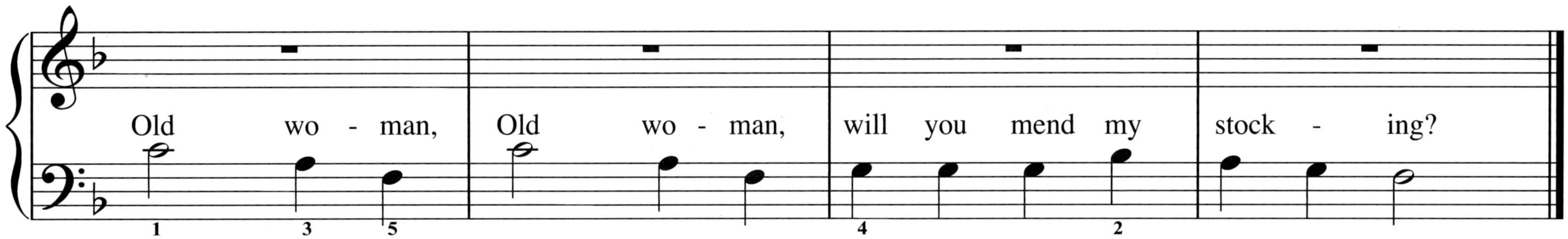

OLD WOMAN
(Variation)

4. Each day change a few notes to create a new variation.

5. Transpose to G and Gb Major.

COME AND JOIN ME

A *sequence* is a melodic pattern repeated on a higher or lower tone. Find all of the *sequences* in this song.

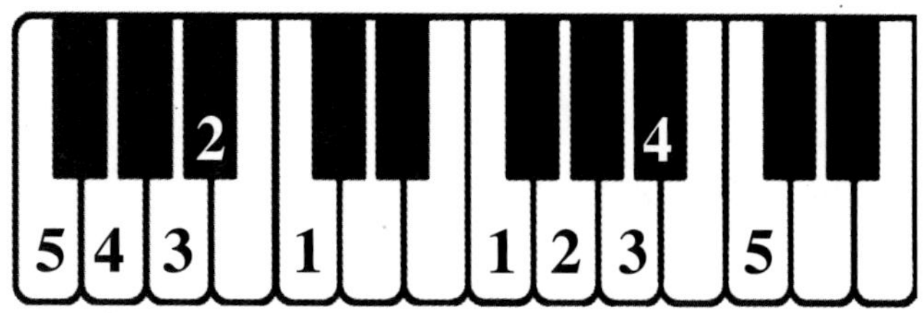

COME AND JOIN ME

Play this song in D Major, then transpose it to Db and Eb Major. Watch for the patterns and sequences.

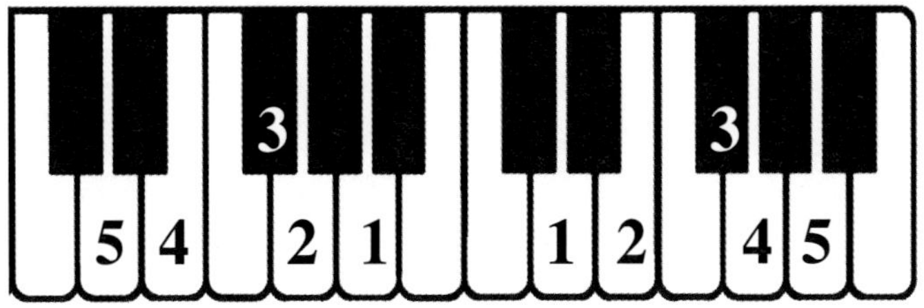

SCANDINAVIAN FOLK SONG

TINKER

1. "Tune up" by playing the first five tones in the key of C Major to find the starting tone. Notice where this melody has repeated tones, steps and skips.

Key of C Major

SLOVAK FOLK SONG

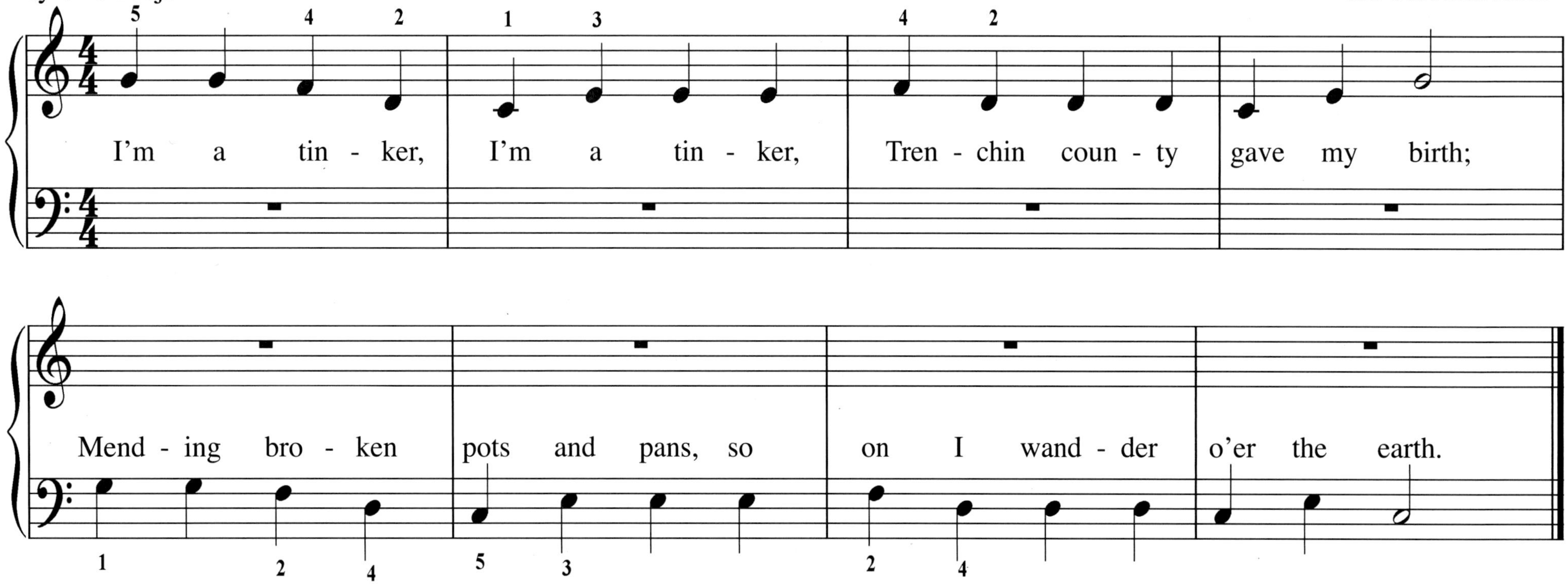

STOP AND GO

2. Be sure to hold the dotted half notes three counts--wait for the "stop light!"

Key of F Major

3. Transpose to E and G Major

BOUNCING

1. The accent mark (>) tells us to make that note a little louder than the others.

PLAYING TOGETHER

2. Before playing this, look for the patterns and try either hand alone on the five black keys.

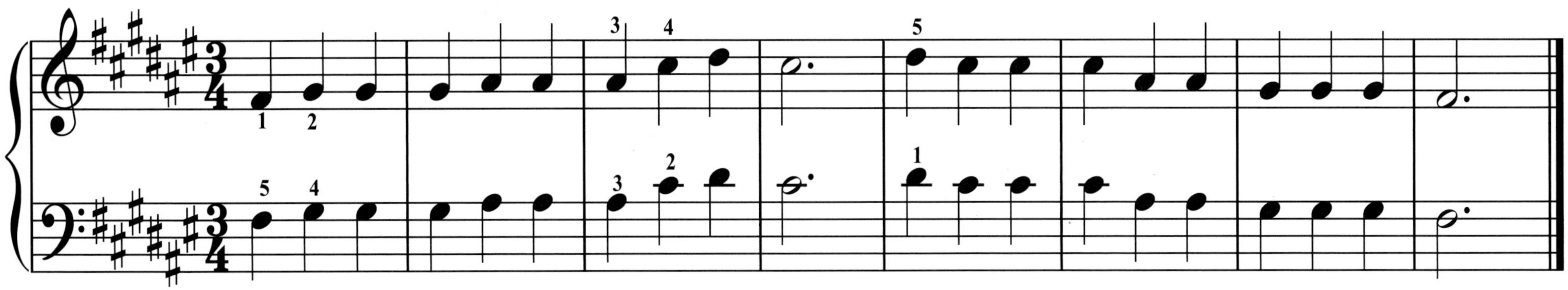

3. Transpose to G Major

WHISTLE DAUGHTER

This melody has repeated tones, steps and skips. Count aloud (quar-ter, quar-ter, etc) and notice the dynamics.

FOLK SONG

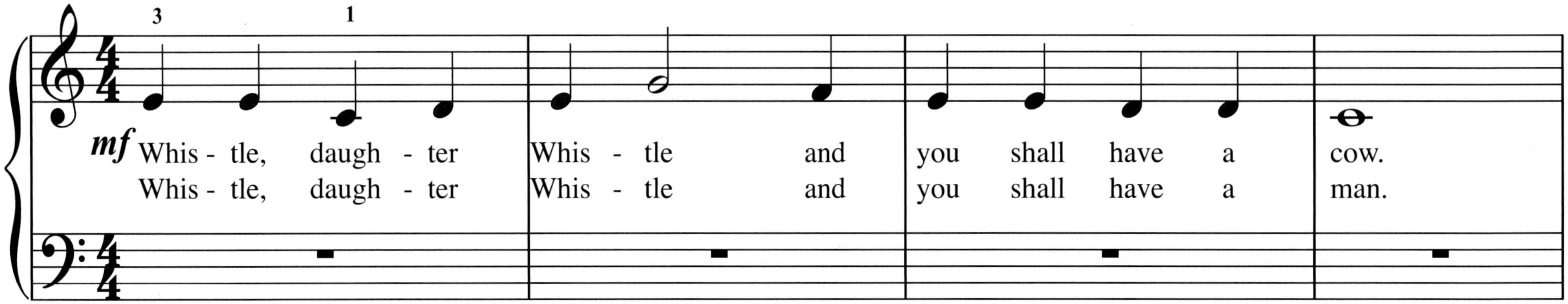

mf (mezzo-forte) means "medium loud"

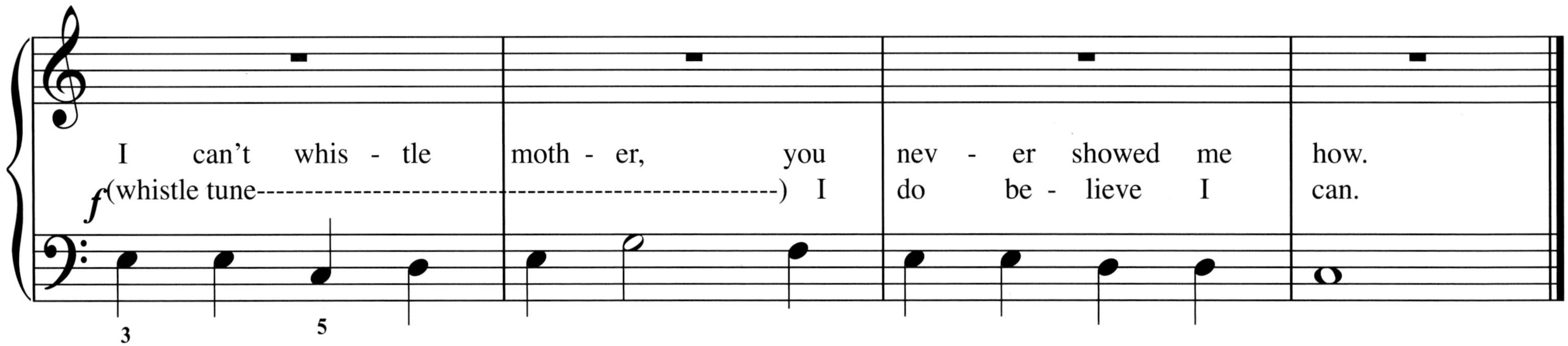

f (forte) means "loud"

WHISTLE DAUGHTER

(Variation)

Circle the places that are different from "Whistle Daughter" on page 18, then play this "Variation." Next, change a few notes to create your own variation.

LIGHTLY ROW

Two eighth notes get the same time as one quarter note.

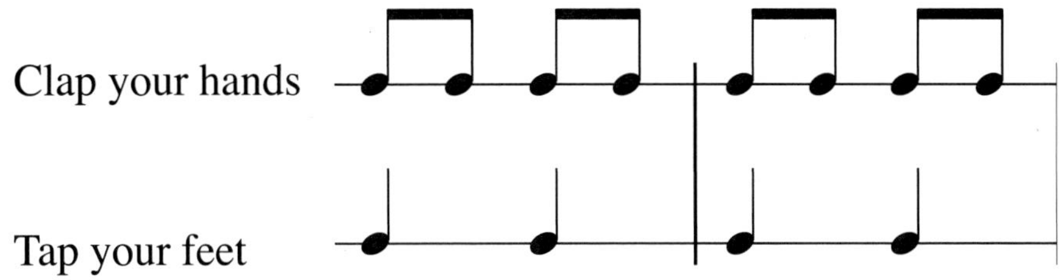

ENGLISH FOLK SONG

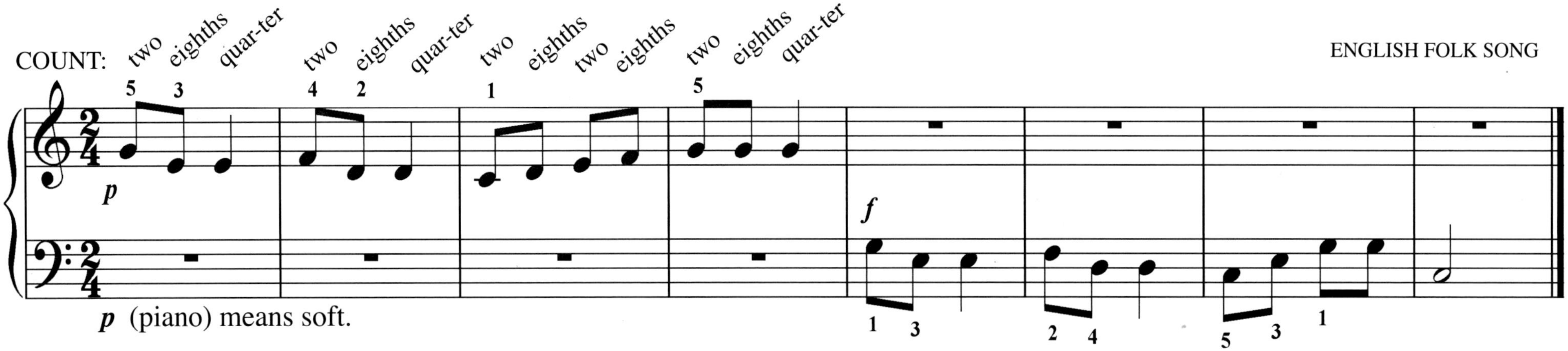

p (piano) means soft.

SONG

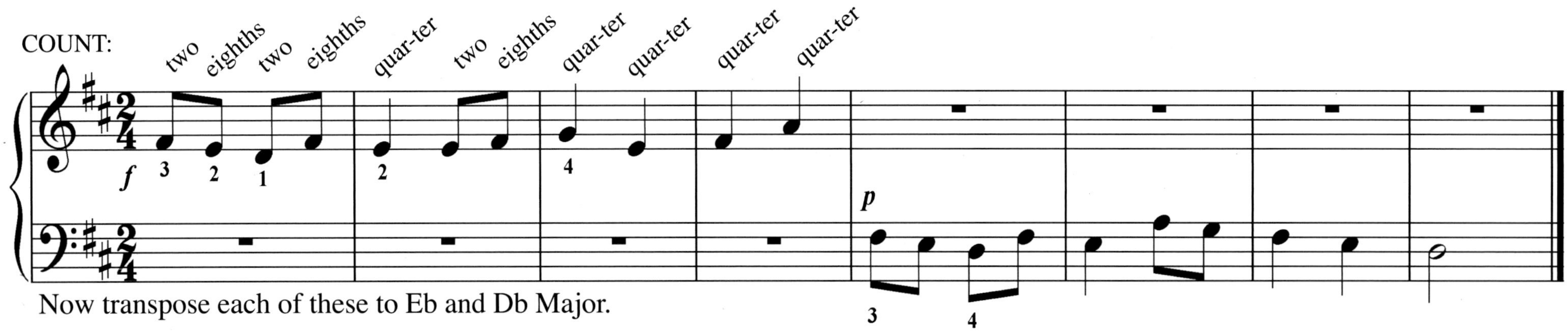

Now transpose each of these to Eb and Db Major.

WALTZ MELODY

1. Find all melodic and rhythmic patterns.
2. Can you find the skip?
3. Count: two eighths, quar-ter, quar-ter.

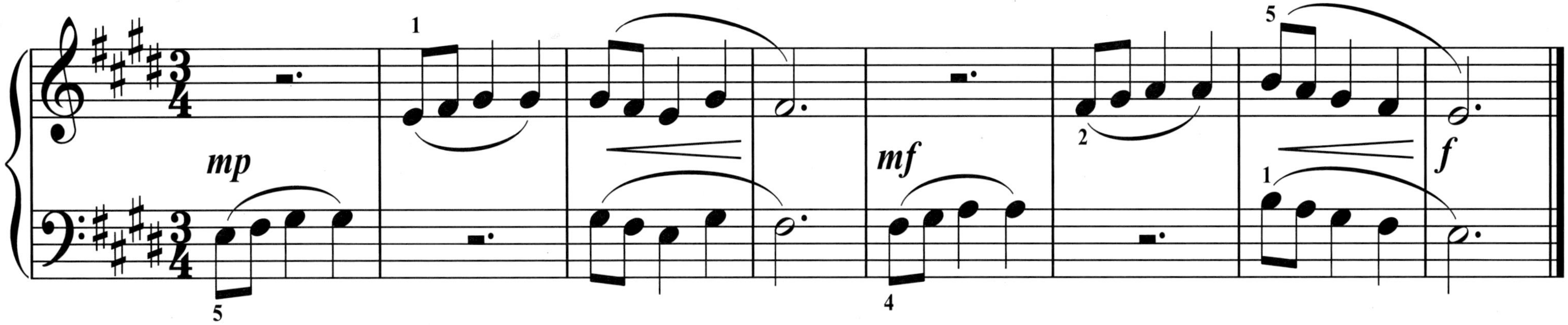

PUZZLE SONG

This melody is a puzzle. Find the following:
1. Where the melody is inverted (upside down).
2. Where the melody pattern is repeated.

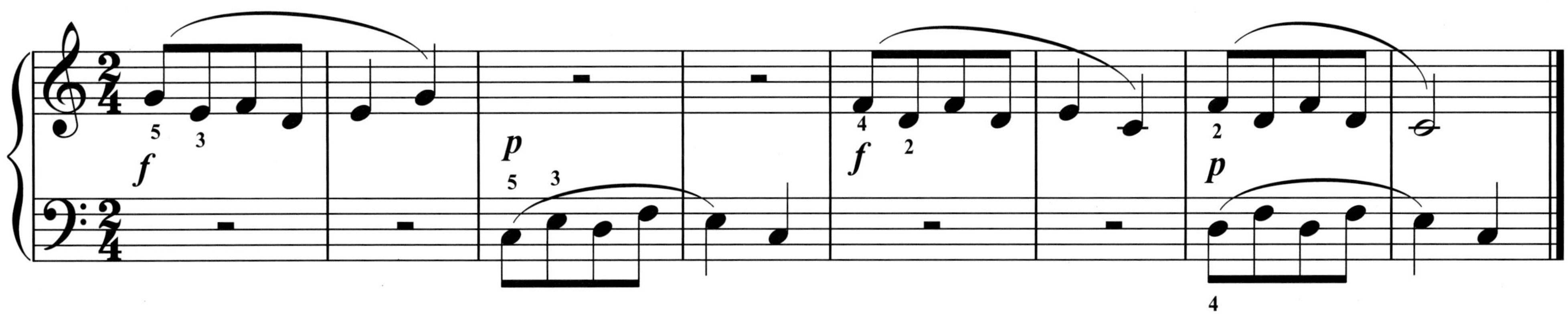

Eighth notes may be grouped in two's or four's as in these two songs.

CASEY JONES

AMERICAN TUNE
(Adapted)

1. Count (quar-ter, quar-ter, half note) as you play this song.

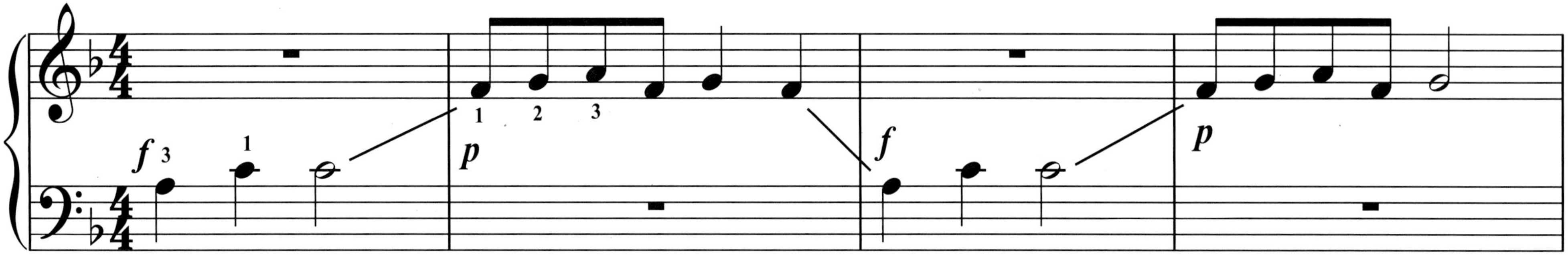

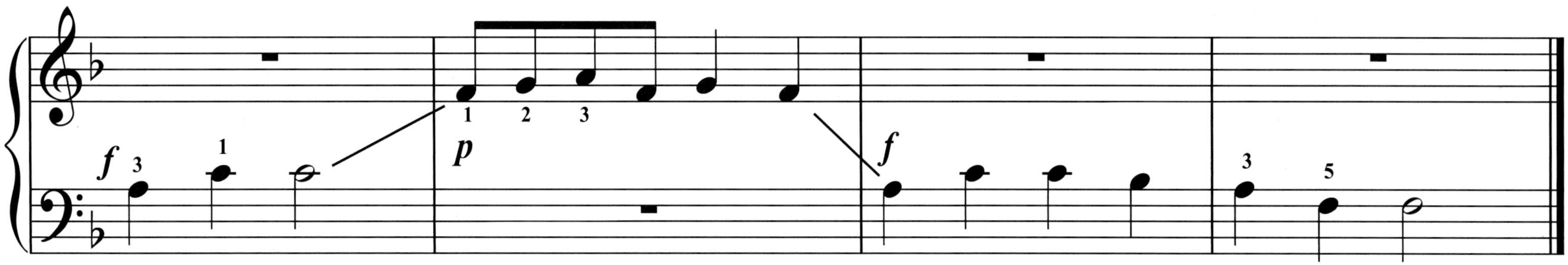

VARIATION

2. The curved lines called slurs show you each *phrase* of music. This means get louder (crescendo) and this means get softer (decrescendo).

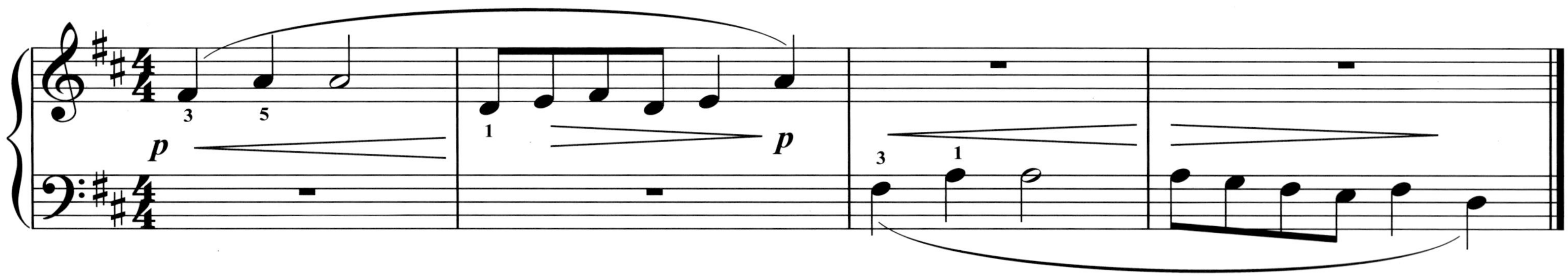

QUESTION AND ANSWER

1. In music, the first phrase (4 bars) often asks a "Question" and the second phrase (4 bars) gives an "Answer." Here is an example:

2. Here is the same Question with a different Answer.

3. Now use this same Question and create your own Answers. Use the same three notes to begin your Answer and end on G.

Be sure to see ***Creative Music*** and ***Theory Papers*** for more examples of this Question and Answer.

4. Play this new Question and Answer, then create some of your own.

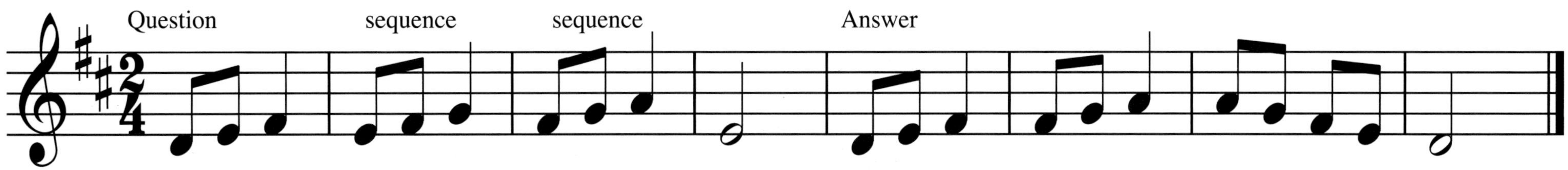

PENTATONIC DUET

This duet is built on the *Pentatonic Scale* (five notes). Learn both parts of this duet and also make up new melodies for the right hand.

ANCIENT DANCE

Notice that the 1st and 3rd parts of this are similar. The 2nd part (B) has a different melody and rhythm. The fermata (𝄐) tells you to hold that note longer.

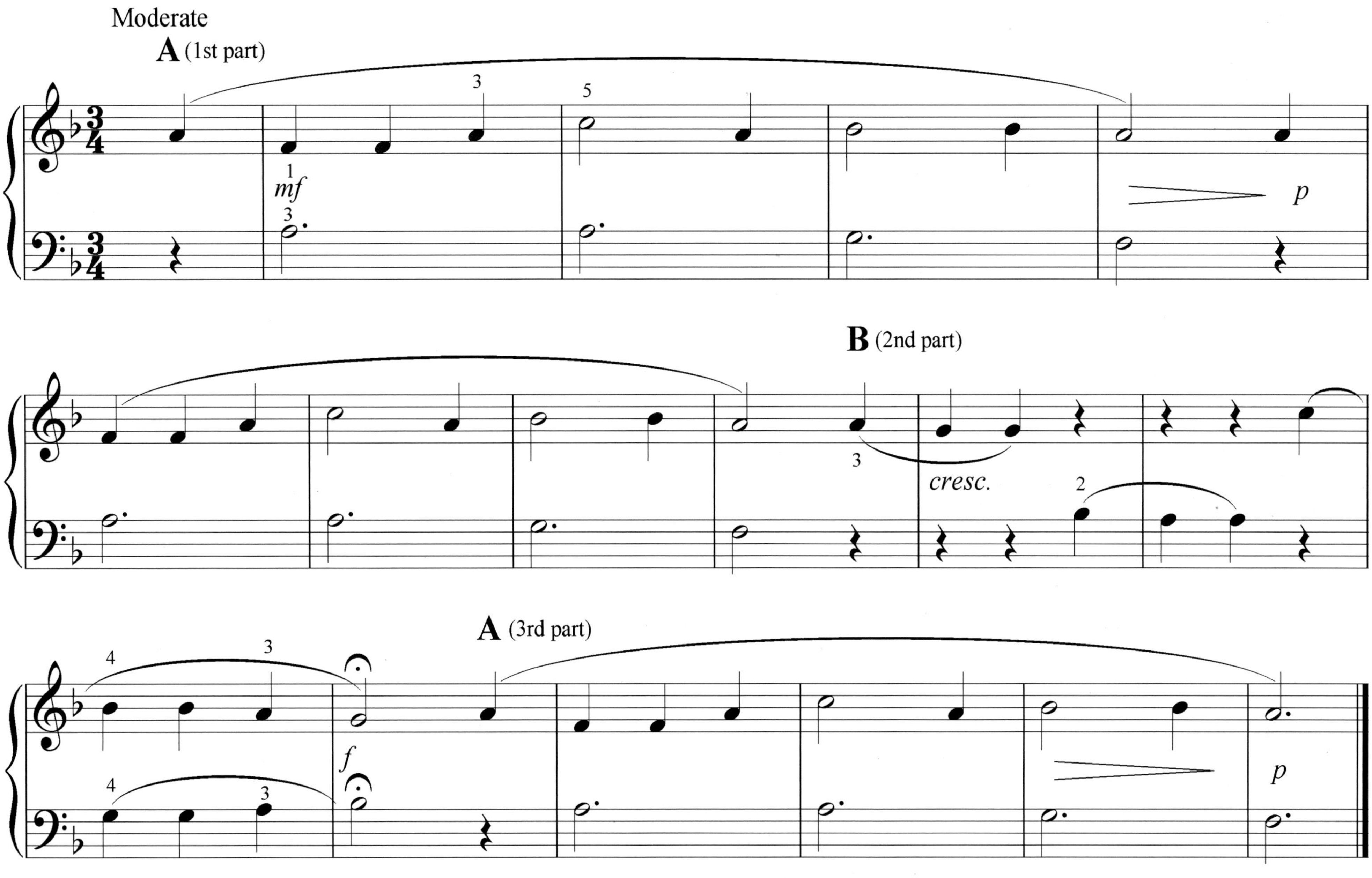

LIGHTLY HOP

1. A staccato mark makes a note half of its regular length. Use a "down-up" (pecking) motion of the wrist to play each note.

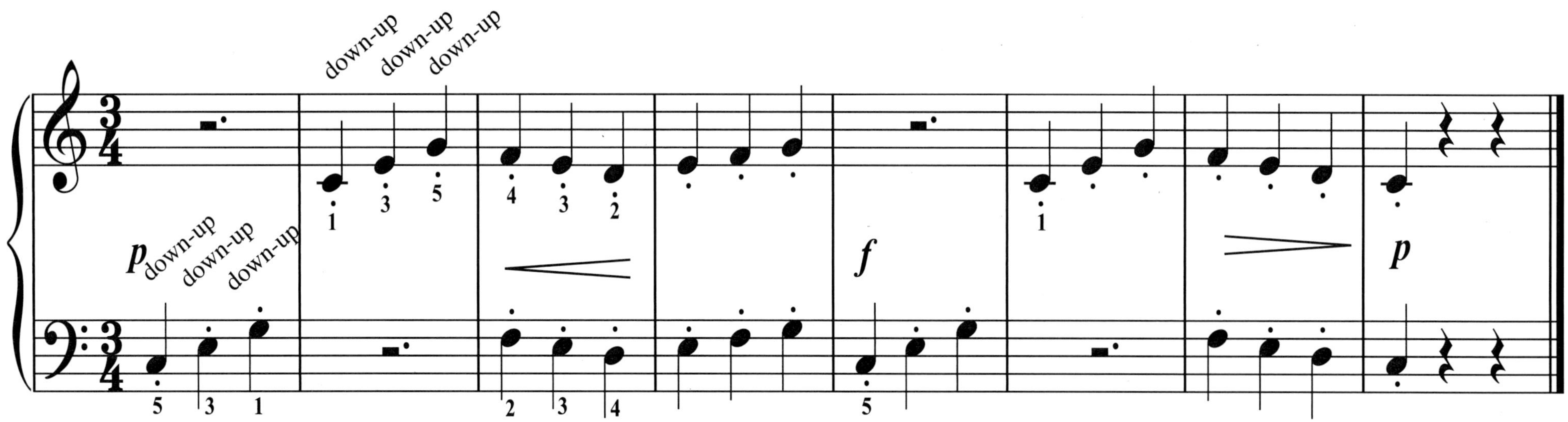

STACCATO STUDY

2. First, play this slowly with a very exact "down-up" motion for each note. Gradually play it faster.

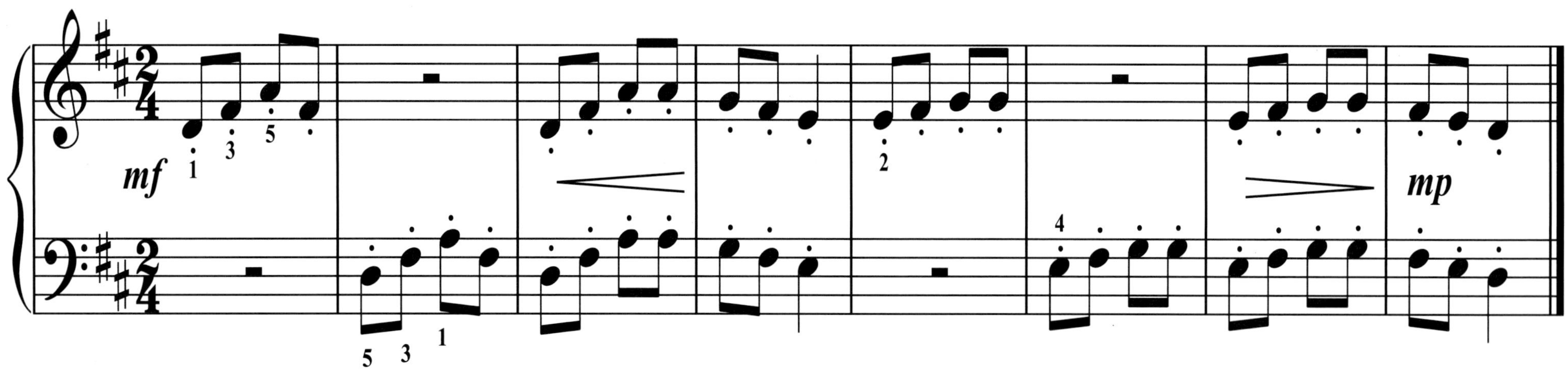

CHORD SONGS

Three tones played together are called a triad or *chord*. 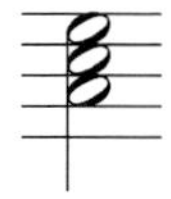

1. The Chord Songs beginning on C, F and G use white keys only

C Major

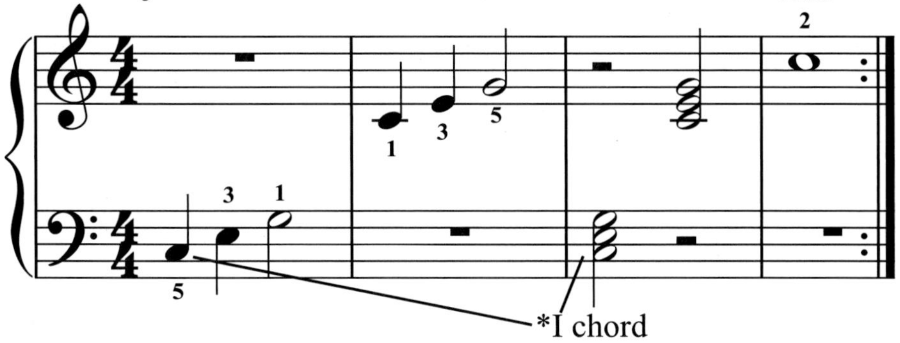

F Major

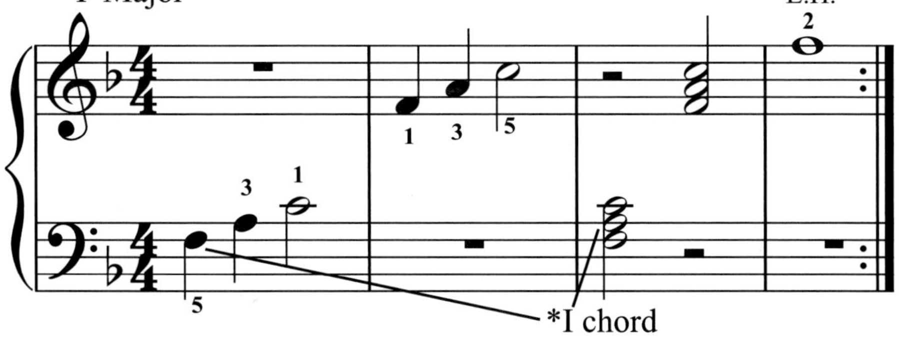

G Major

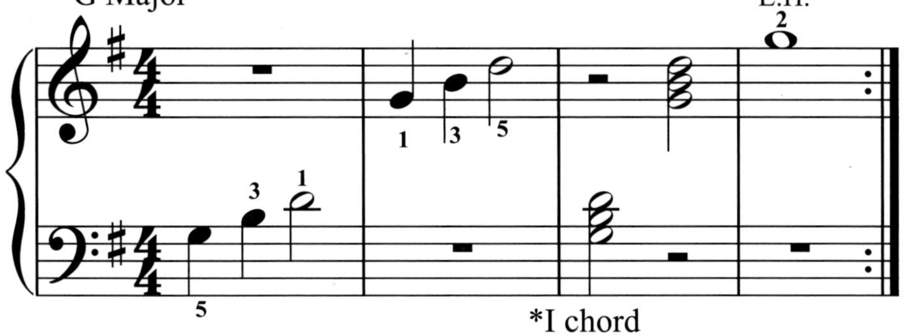

2. The Chord Songs beginning on D, E and A have a black key in the middle.

D Major

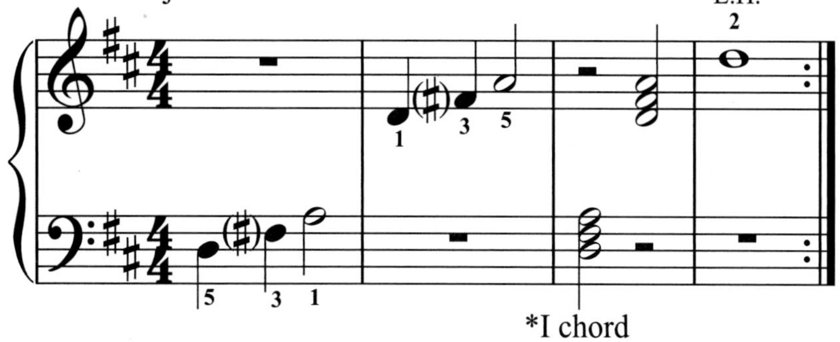

E Major

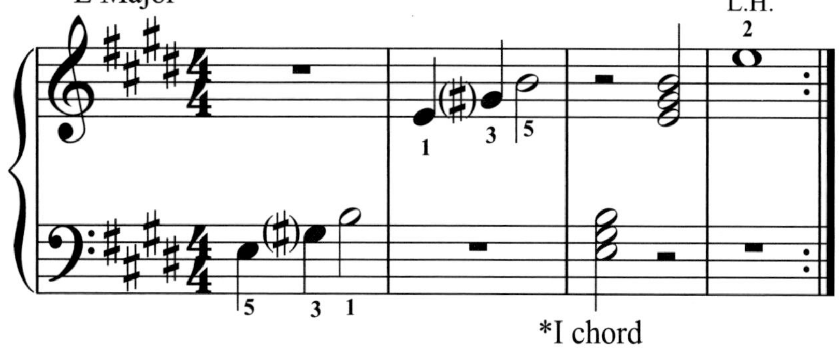

A Major

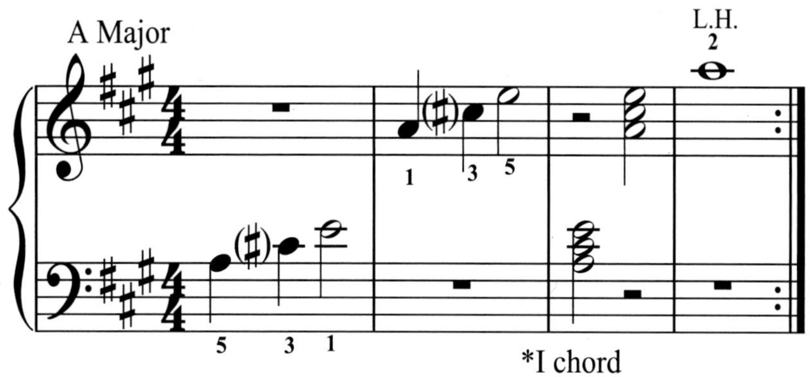

*These chords are called "One Chords" (I) because the bottom note of each chord is the first tone of that key.

ETUDE

1. Here, we play melody and harmony together. This melody is made up of tones from the I chord (they are called "chord tones"). Play the chord in the left hand, as you slowly sample the melody notes in the right hand. Notice these are the same tones in both hands. Practice each day letting your eye follow the shape of the melody as you also see the chord in the bass.

2. Now play the chords in the right hand and the melody in the left hand. Watch both parts as you play.

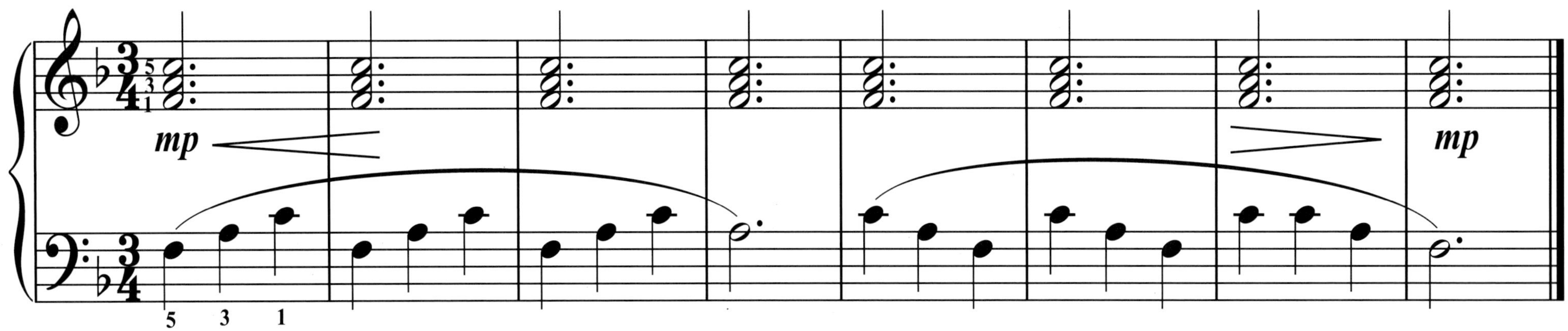

3. Transpose to the keys of Gb and G Major.

CHORD SONGS

1. The Db, Eb and Ab Major chords each have a white key in the middle.

Db Major

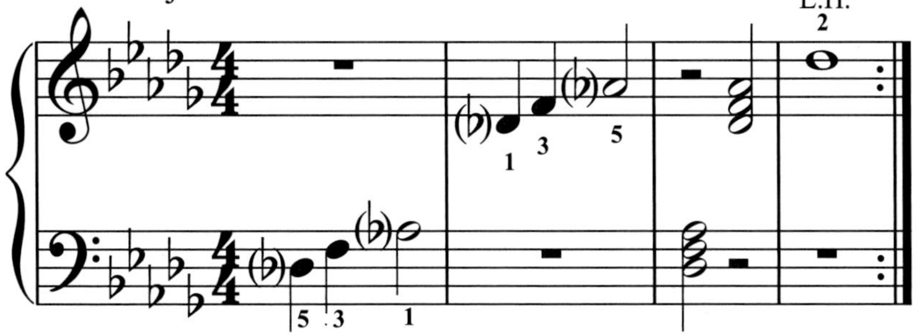

I chord

Eb Major

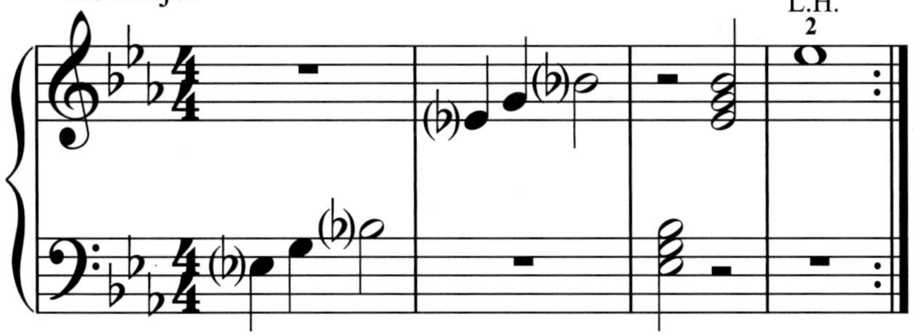

I chord

Ab Major

I chord

2. Each of the three remaining chords is different. Gb is all black, Bb has one black key on the bottom, B Major has black keys on the middle and top notes.

Gb Major

I chord

Bb Major

I chord

B Major

I chord

MARCH

Here is a new chord called the Dominant 7th or V7. The top note stays while the middle note moves up and the bottom note moves down. Try first in C Major then transpose to Db and D Major.

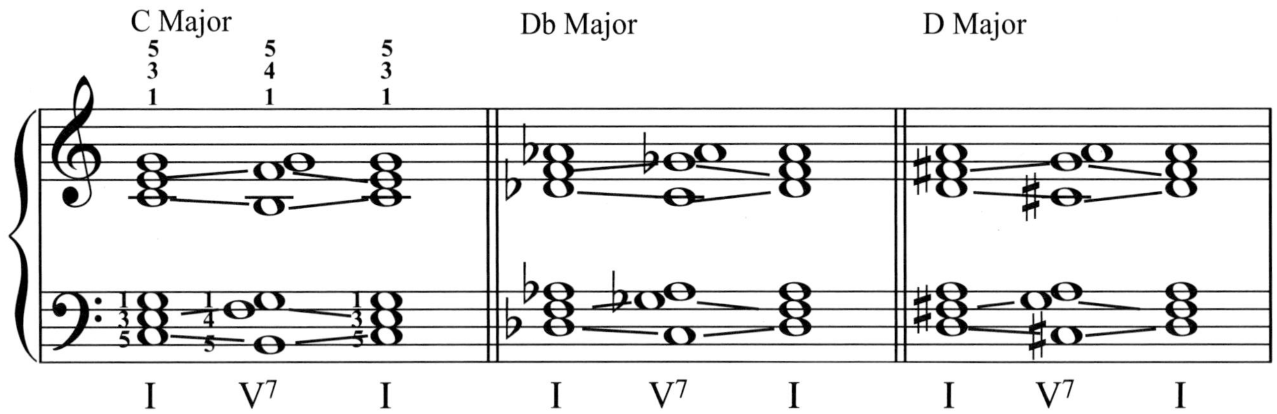

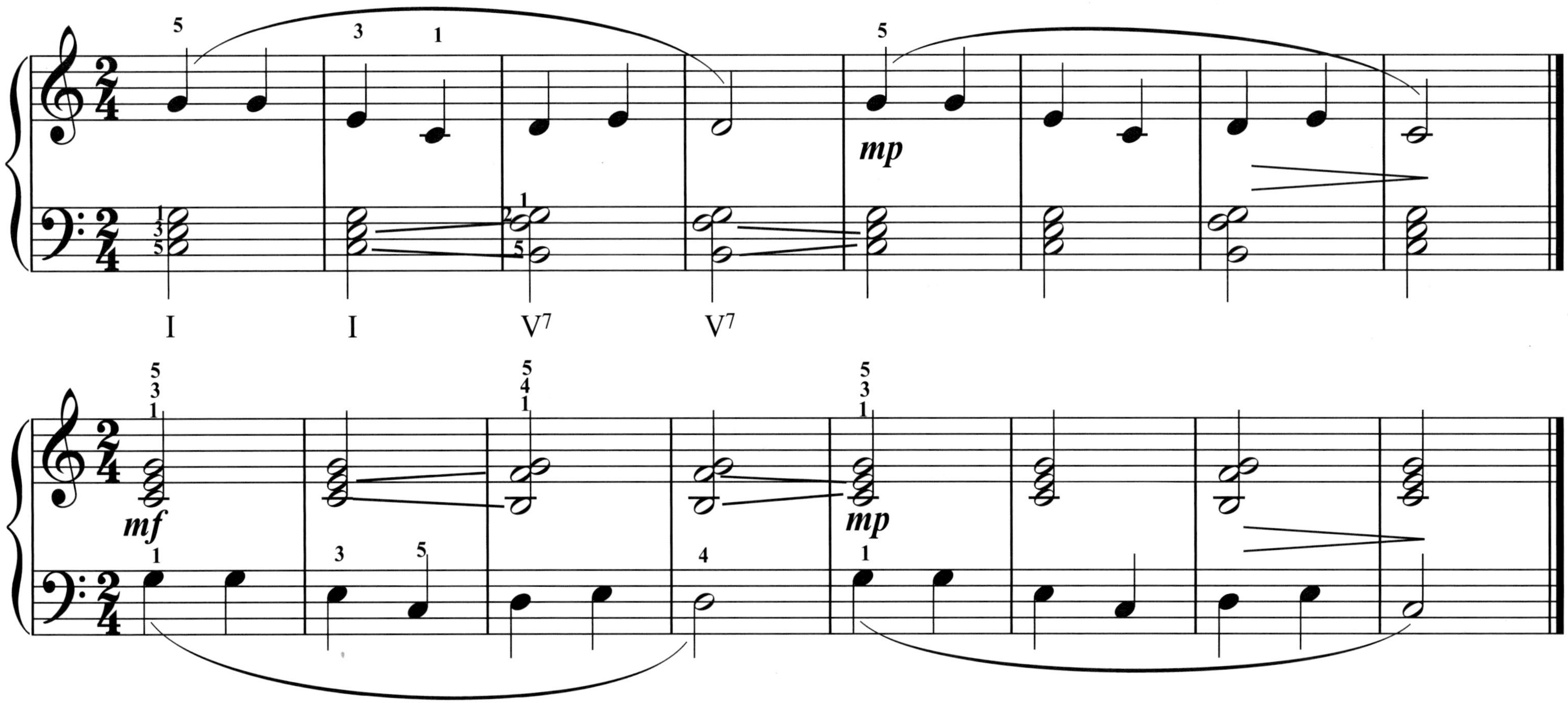

SAILING

1. The melody of "Sailing" is made up of chord tones of the I and V7 chords. Notice that it moves mainly by skips. Look for any repeated patterns.

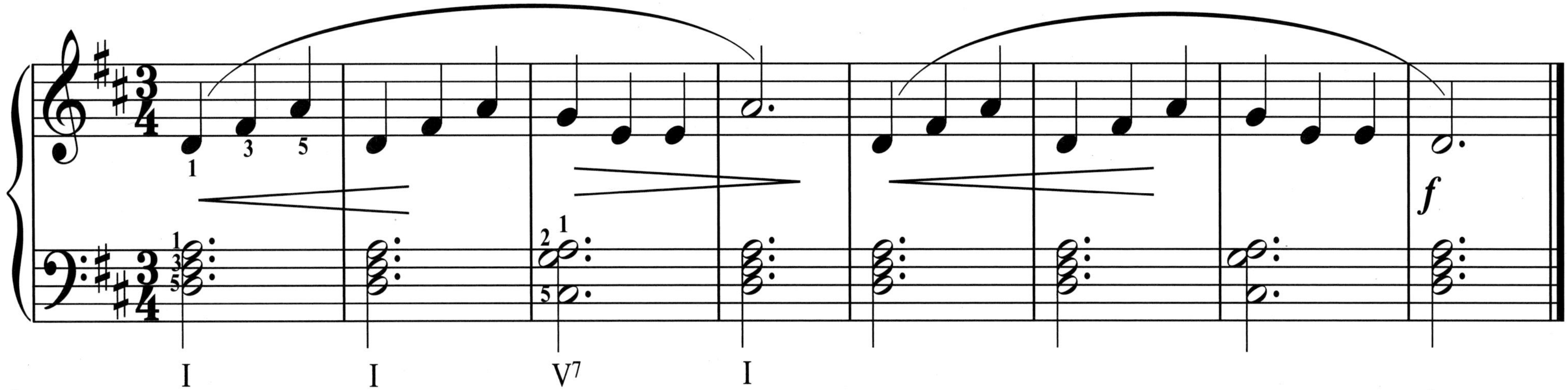

2. Transpose to Eb and E Major

SUBMARINE

3. Here the melody moves by steps except in the 2nd and 6th measures. Transpose to Db and D Major.

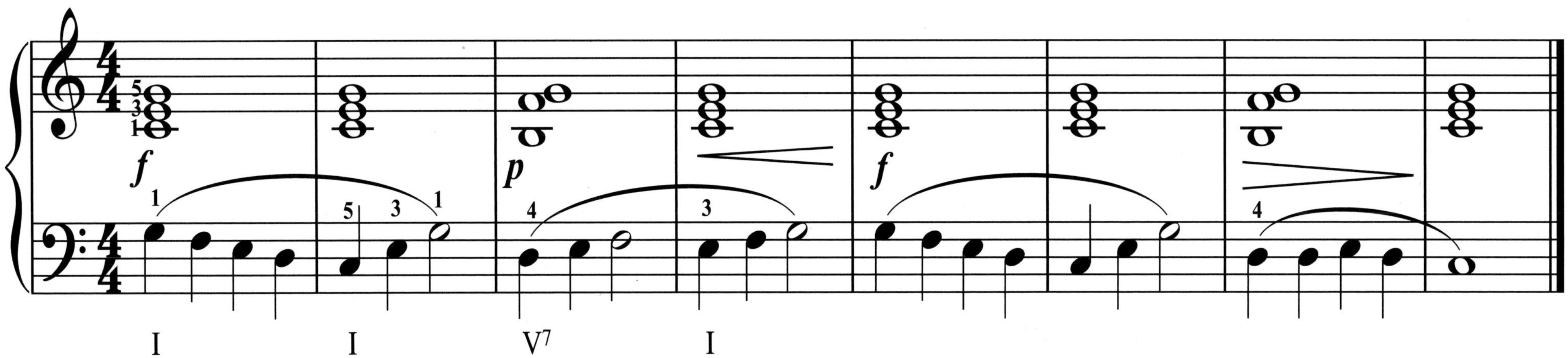

DOTTED NOTES

The dot placed beside a note lengthens it by one half its original length. A good way to get the correct rhythm is to sing or say the note names as you play the melody.

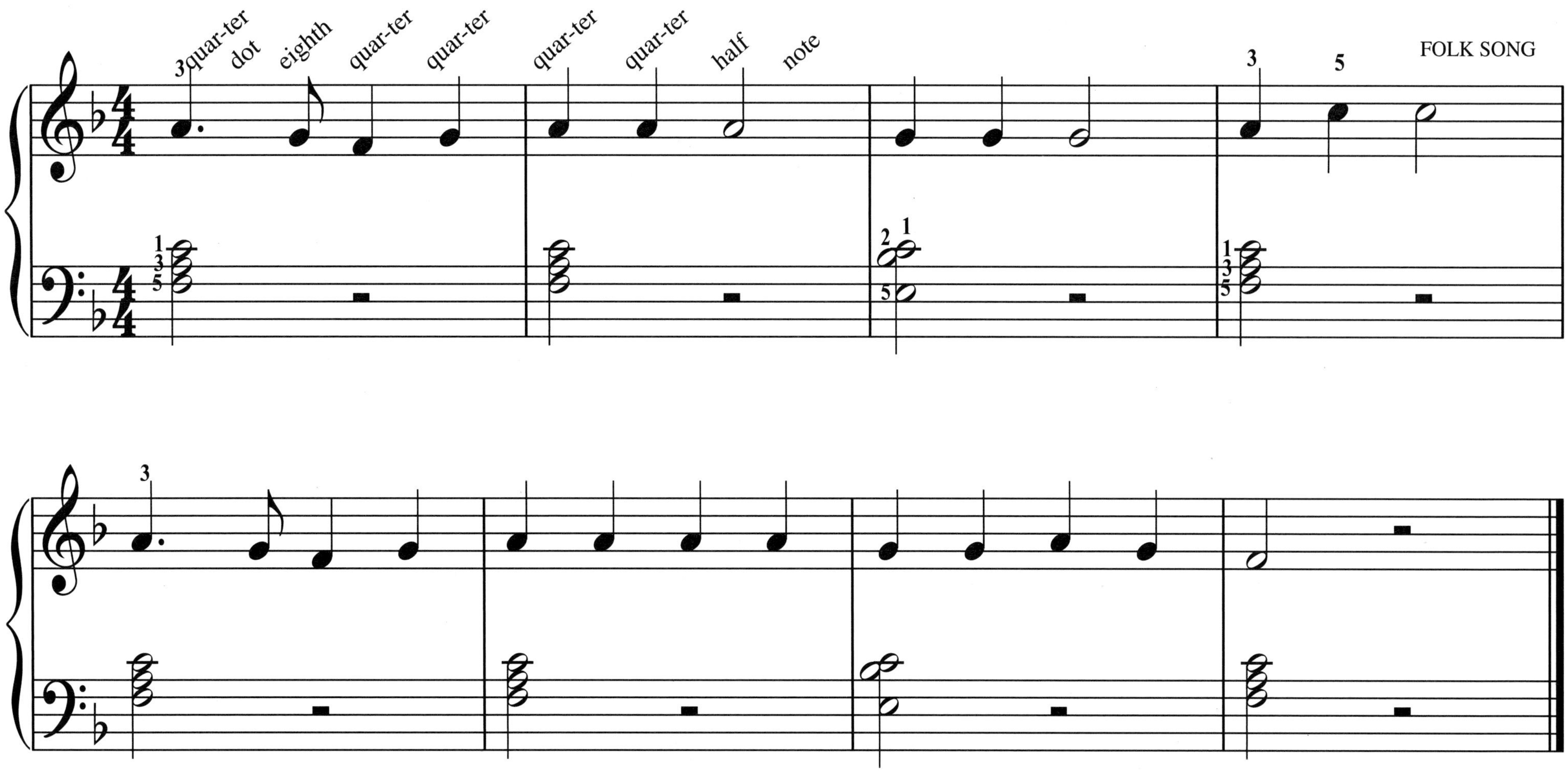

TIP TOES

A staccato mark shortens the note by one half of its usual length. So, a staccato quarter note is the same length as an eighth note followed by an eighth rest (♩ = ♪𝄾). Practice “Tip Toes” with a very exact **down-up** “pecking” motion for each note. Gradually, play it faster making sure that each note of the melody has a rest between it and the next one. Transpose to D and C Major.

LOOBY LOO

In $\frac{6}{8}$ meter, there are six counts in each measure and the eighth note gets one count. If you wish to count by numbers, use two groups of three counts in each measure. However, it is easier to count by saying the type of note (eighth note, quar-ter, etc.) as indicated here.

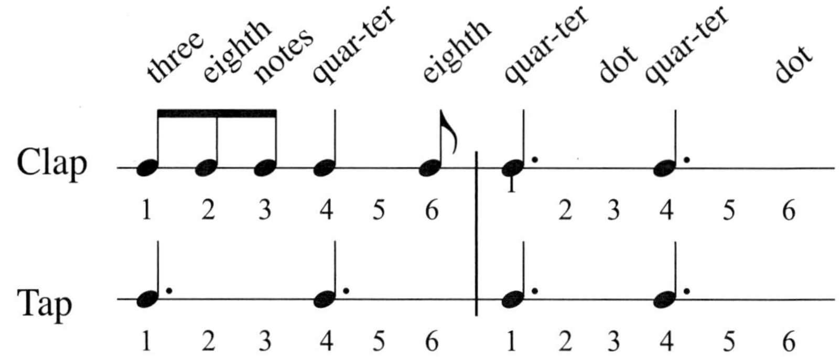

When two notes are tied ( ) do not play the second tone. However, give it the full time value as indicated.

ROW, ROW, ROW YOUR BOAT

Since the second chord is "tied" to the first one, do not play it again. Be sure to give each note its full value by saying, "quar-ter dot, quar-ter dot, etc." Notice where you shift your right hand as you play the melody. Don't stop between the first and second lines.

Transpose to D and E Major.

CONTRASTS

Make lots of contrast between the first two measures (forte) and the second two measures (piano). After playing it as written, try it again with both a waltz bass. Transpose to C and B major.

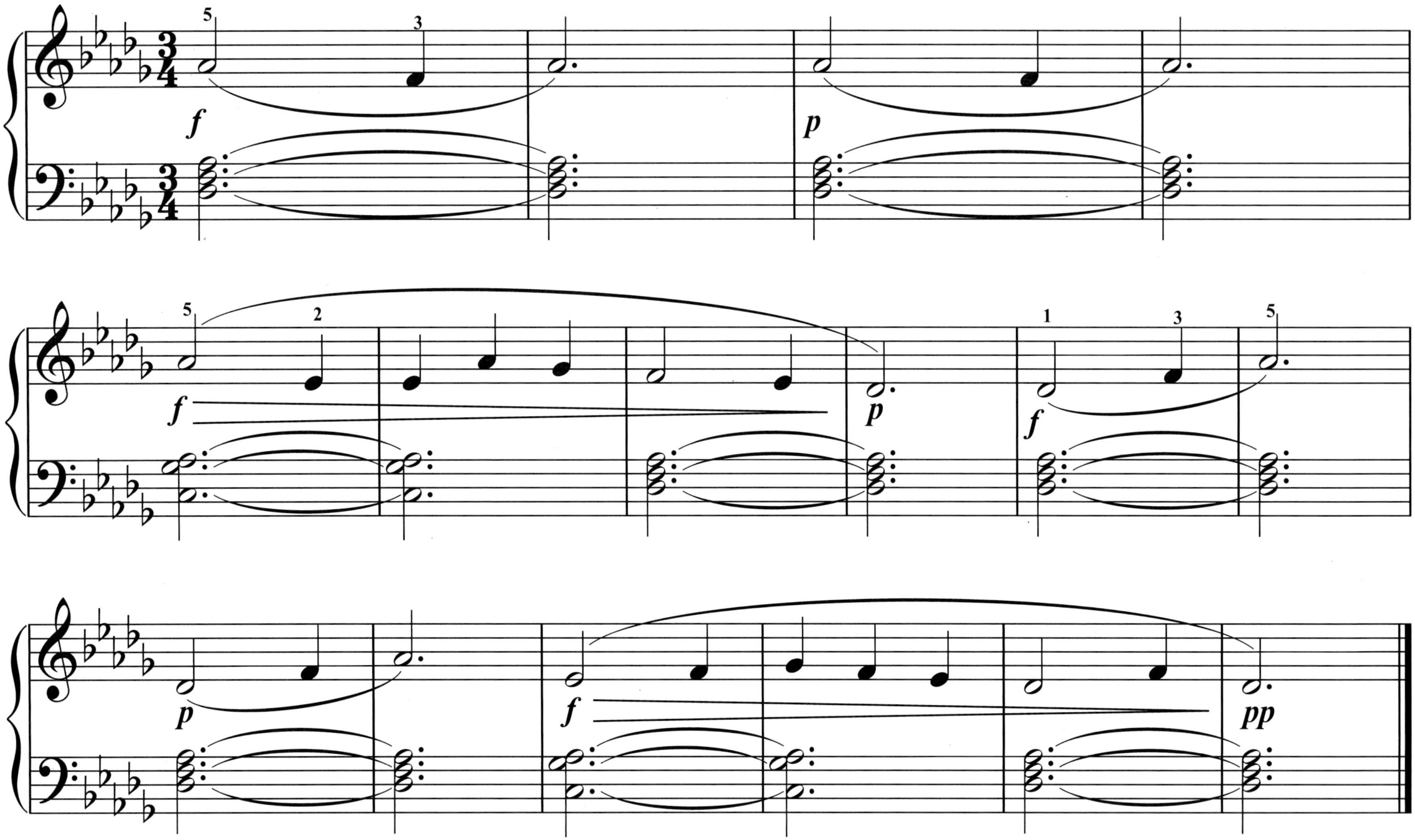

JINGLE BELLS

The left hand uses these four notes: 

J. PIERPONT

STATELY DANCE

1. Look for the sequence in the melody and play the left hand with a down-up motion in each measure. Transpose to E and F Major.

Repeat softly one octave higher.

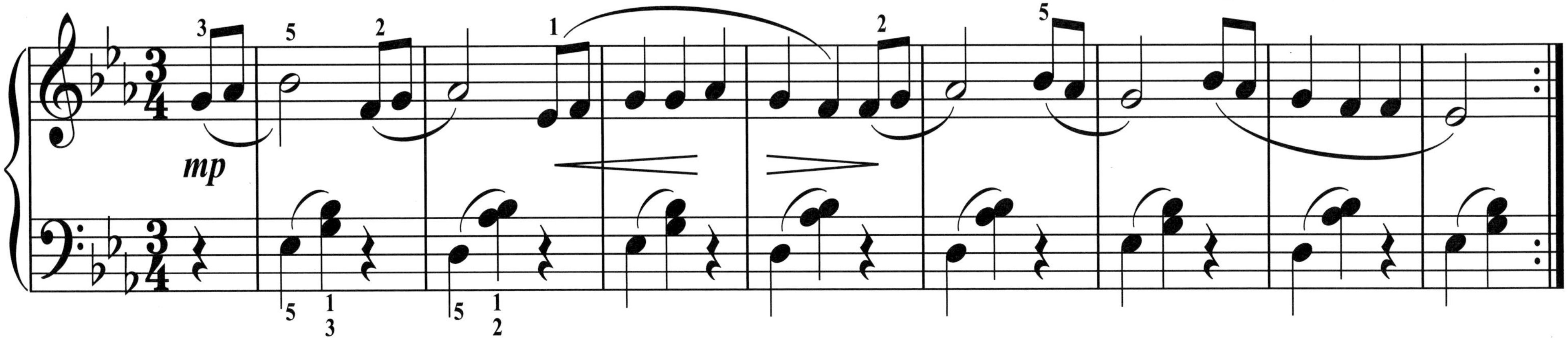

2. Here is another melody with the same left hand pattern. Create other melodies with this same rhythm and chord pattern.

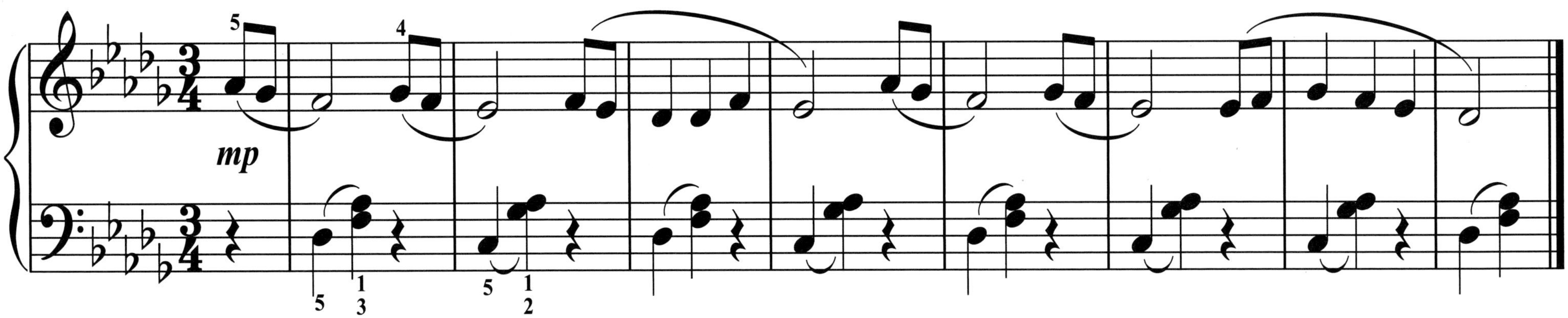

TWINKLE, TWINKLE

Learn both parts of this duet.

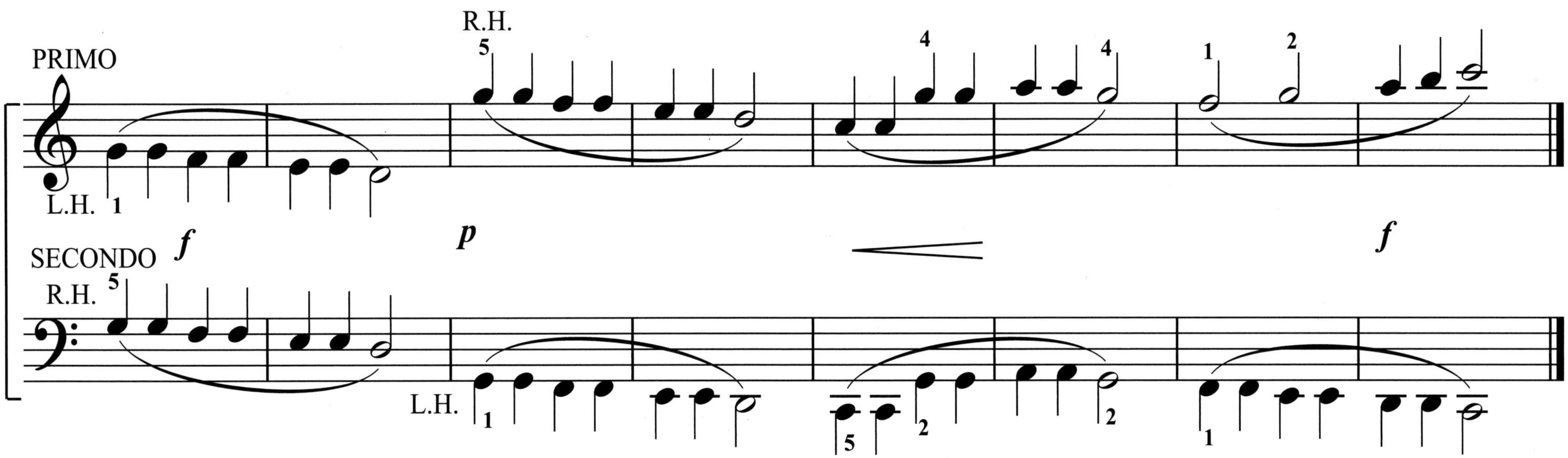

MINOR CHORDS

A major chord (triad) becomes minor when the middle note is lowered one half step (the next closest tone). Play these Major and minor chords, then practice naming others with your "Major Triads" and "Minor Triads" flashcards.

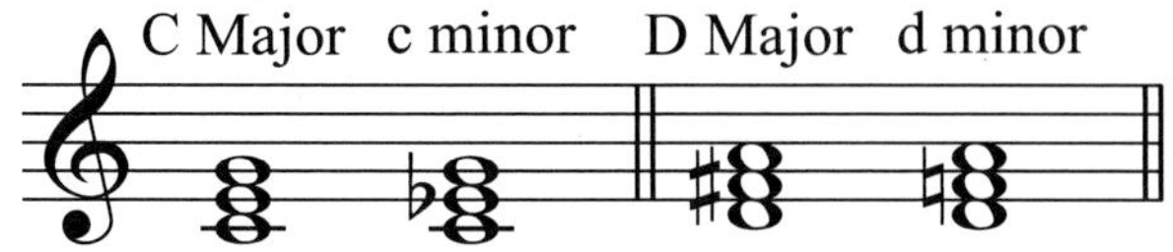

RELATIVE MAJOR AND MINOR

Major and minor keys that share the same signature are called *relative* Major and minor. They have different letter names.

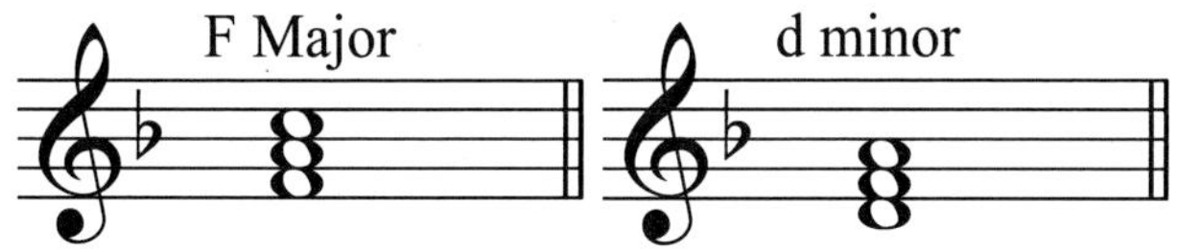

1. First play this melody in F Major.

2. Now play this in its *relative* minor key (d minor).

PARALLEL MAJOR AND MINOR

Major and minor keys with the same letter name (such as D Major and d minor) are called *parallel* major and minor. They have different key signatures. See page 50 of "Musical Games and Activities to play interesting games with your "Minor Triads" and "Key Signatures" flash cards.

LULLABY

Play "Lullaby" first in D Major and then in its parallel key, d minor. Notice that the V7 chord is the same for both.

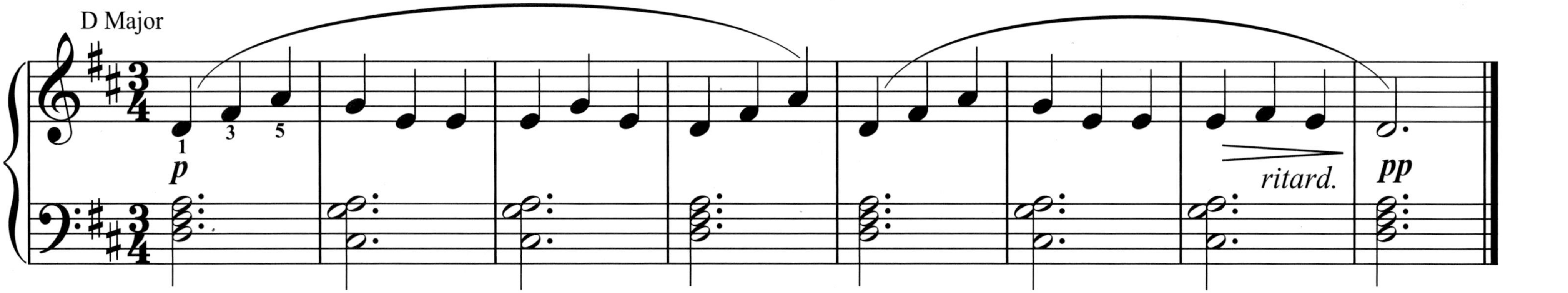

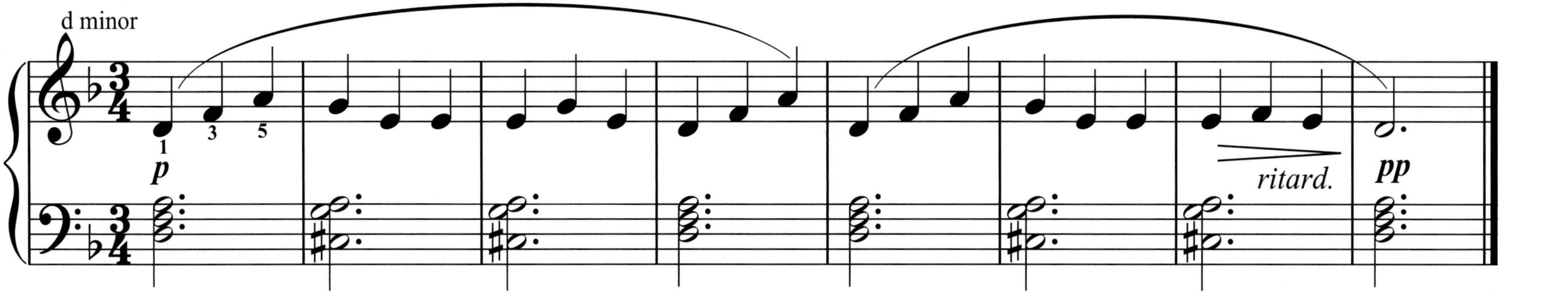

For more drill on relative and parallel minor see ***Theory Papers***.

SURPRISES

Notice the V7 chord is the same in both Major and minor.

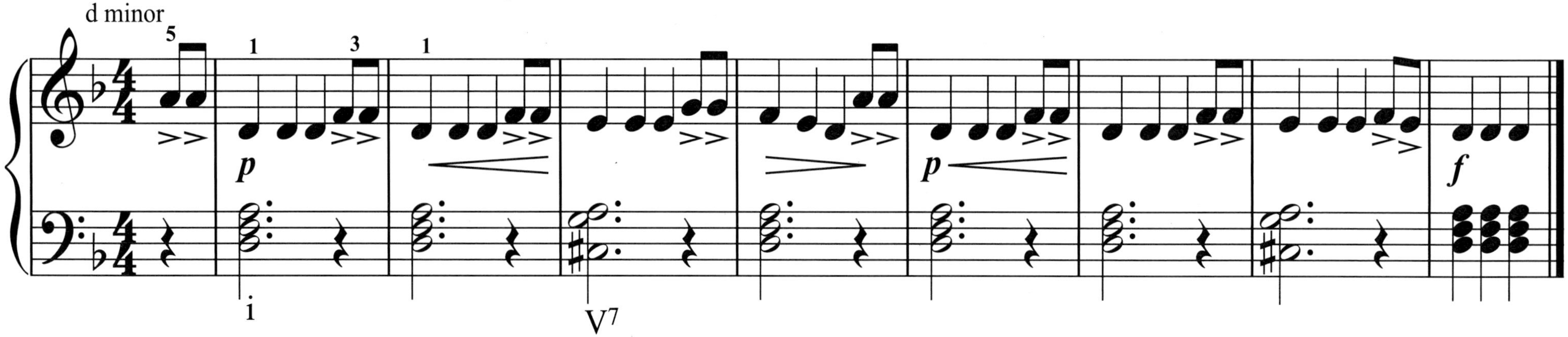

GOBLINS

Transpose to g minor.

JIG

This piece in Dorian mode uses the white keys from D to D. Try different fingering in the right hand to find the best for you.

CONCERT TIME

1. Play the left hand "Alberti" bass much softer than the right hand melody.

2. First play "Spring Dance" as written.
Then try it with your own variations.

SPRING DANCE

SOUNDING DRUMS, NEAR AND FAR

Observe the repeat sign in measure six. After playing as written, create your own "pentatonic dances."

PARADE

You may play only the top notes in the right hand or you may play both as written. Make a gradual crescendo from the beginning to the second line of page 47. Then get softer and fade out at the end.

f
ff
f
mp
gradually slower and fade out
p
ppp

ACHIEVEMENT TEST

1. Sightread this melody then harmonize it.

2. Write the correct time signatures and play each example.

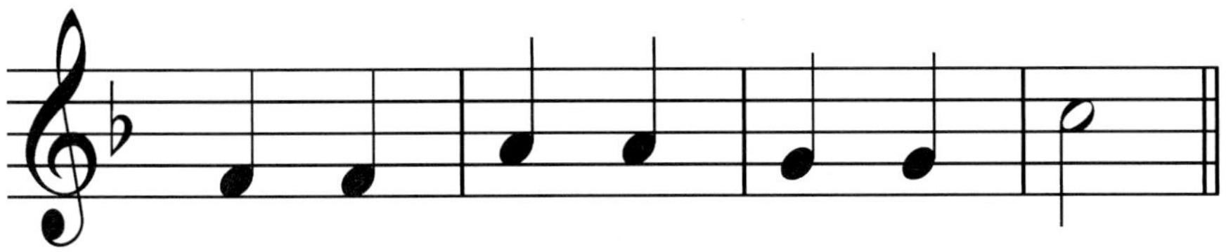

3. Write the correct key signatures.

E Major Db Major d minor

E Major Db Major d minor

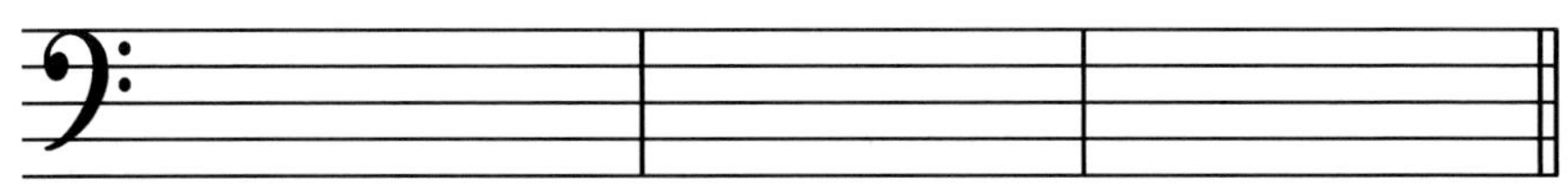

4. Play this question and make up an answer.

Question Answer

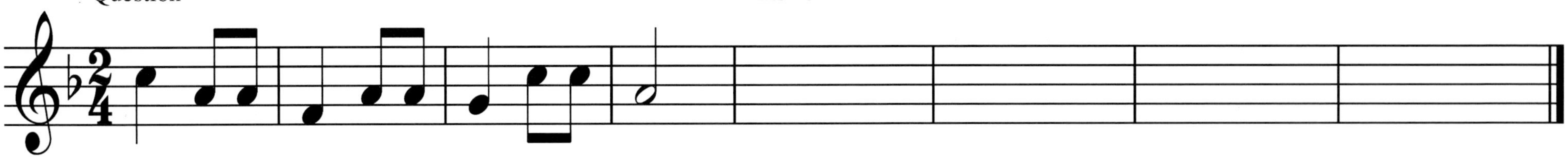